POSTCARDS
FROM THE COUNTRY

POSTCARDS
From the Country

LIVING MEMORIES OF THE
BRITISH COUNTRYSIDE

PETER MARREN &
MIKE BIRKHEAD

BBC BOOKS

ACKNOWLEDGEMENTS

Postcards from the Country relies on the memories of its
many contributors. We thank the production team who researched
each area, and found our story tellers. They are: Vanessa Berlowitz,
Phil Chapman, Karen Hewson, Anthony Lee, Karen Partridge,
David Rolfe and Alison Tancock. We also thank Linda Blakemore
for the design, Susannah Playfair for the picture research,
and Sheila Ableman and Anna Ottewill for steering the
book to its conclusion.

This book is published to accompany the BBC television series entitled
Postcards from the Country which was first broadcast in 1996
and produced by Mike Birkhead.

Published by BBC Books, an imprint of BBC Worldwide Publishing,
BBC Worldwide Limited, 80 Wood Lane, London W12 OTT.

First published 1996
© Peter Marren and Michael Birkhead 1996
ISBN 0 563 37157 9

Set in Plantin Light by BBC Books
Printed and bound in Great Britain by Butler & Tanner Limited, Frome
Colour separations by Radstock Reproductions Limited, Midsomer Norton
Jacket printed by Lawrence Allen Limited, Weston-super-Mare

CONTENTS

FOREWORD

In *Pig Earth*, his tribute to Europe's vanishing peasants, John Berger argues that what gives rural communities their special character is the telling of stories. Stories of the distant past and of what happened that same day. A village is continuously making 'a living portrait of itself: a communal portrait, in that everybody is portrayed and everybody portrays.' The fact that gossip – in the best sense – is still a vital ingredient of the blood-flow of the countryside is demonstrated in these despatches.

What is recalled in them from 'living memory' is also living in another sense. These stories are proud, vivid, intensely local. They expect responses or sequels. Some seem almost to be parables, and to define a moment in time or the character of a place. Cornish fishermen, harvesting violets and daffodils; their wives salting pilchards on the harbour-front and making 'flowers' of pilchards to top-off the barrels: they could be images from a medieval Book of Hours.

But there is an elegiac note here too. Many of the stories sound like memorials as much as memories, reflecting a belief that things will never be the same again, that the countryside is changing faster and more dramatically than it has for two centuries. In the Yorkshire Dales ramblers outnumber not only shepherds but sheep. The punts of Norfolk Broads reed-cutters have been replaced by pleasure cruisers. Even in the remote redoubts of the Cairngorms, mobile phones ring from climbers' rucksacks. Everywhere the 'incomer' – that much-demonized figure in rural mythology – has acquired a new, ambivalent importance not least because he or she is often the person 'carrying on' the stories.

It is a reasonable bet that within two or three decades farming, as we understand it today, will have become a minority land-use in the countryside. And as it contracts, so one of the great seasonal engines that drove and ordered rural communities will run down. It is hard not to view this as an irreparable loss, the breaking of bonds between people and land that were forged over a millennium. What will the countryside be, if not the place where farming happens?

But the changes under way are not a simple story of decline and fall. The poverty and feudalism that are frequent parts of these living memories may also be seeing their last days. So might rural depopulation. Increasing numbers of incomers are genuine new villagers, building communities of craftspeople, small-holders and homeworkers of a kind that would have been unthinkable only a decade ago. And around them there is already the possibility of new, diverse rural landscapes of community forests, organic farms, man-made wetlands. This could be the countryside of the future, a place of re-creation.

But if it is to be more than a playground, it will need continuity – in the land, in communal memory, in those 'living portraits' of itself. These links, between past and present, native and newcomer, can be seen emerging in the stories in this book. Kestrels hunt over the grassy relics of mine-tips near Aberfan. Charcoal is burned again in Kentish coppices – to supply fuel for the incomers' barbecues. These are new workings of familiar rural fables. But they are rightly called 'postcards', because they are messages out of the countryside signalling that its future is a vital, liberating inheritance for all of us.

Richard Mabey

INTRODUCTION

During the past half-century, rural life in England, Scotland and Wales has experienced profound change. Many of us remember scenes that no longer exist, like horse-drawn ploughs, followed by a flock of gulls and lapwings, or stooks of hay drying in the sun. Those whose memories predate the Second World War will recall village streets full of useful shops (not knick-knacks for tourists) and empty of cars. Older people may tell you of a time when even buses were unknown, and when the village was not only a dwelling place but the stage for most of life. They will remind you that the countryside was greener and more pleasant then, that country people were mostly poor, but reasonably contented, and that life, somehow, seemed much fuller. Unfortunately it is all true. Though rural living goes on, many of the links between people and country have been broken: farm machinery and the advance of tarmacadam have seen to that. Many of those who live in country villages now travel to work in the town. For better or worse, much of the countryside has been suburbanized.

However, memories of what it used to be like are still vivid. Future generations will look back on our own times as the dividing line between the old and the new. But although there are plenty of local histories and academic accounts of these changes, few of them have been told by the inhabitants themselves. Oral history, with its freshness and authenticity, is the main benefit that television has brought to the chronicling of recent times. The *Postcards* team travelled to eight contrasting parts of Britain to talk to as broad a range of people as possible who have lived there for much or all of their lives. Over the months we interviewed more than a thousand people, only a fraction of whom can be included here. Their testimonies reveal the extraordinary range of activities supported by our ever-varying scenery. We talked to crofters and fishermen, to miners and fruit-pickers, to housewives and naturalists, to lairds and poachers. We also found a host of lesser-known trades, among them a mole-trapper, a reed-harvester, a wood-reeve, a hermit and more than one poet. The stories they told were invariably vivid, often humorous, ever hopeful, but rarely sentimental. In the television series, and in this book, we have aimed to piece together a celebration of the glorious diversity of life in the British countryside. It tells of close personal attachments to particular places, of ways of life that make use of their surroundings without destroying their beauty, and of a natural empathy with our wild neighbours. It is a story in which life and nature are intermingled.

By reading this book, we hope you will feel the wind on the hill, hear the bleat of spring lambs and smell the pondwater on the village green. The great blessing of the age of the family car is that such things are now easy to reach, even for those of us who live in inner cities. We hope that this book will add to your enjoyment and appreciation of our remaining wild places, and provide a sense of the hidden relationships of man and land.

Mike Birkhead and Peter Marren

POSTCARD

— Chapter One —

The Centre of the Universe

A VILLAGE IN KENT

EVERY VILLAGE is at the centre of someone's universe. In part it was because the village used to supply most of the necessities of life, from Holy Communion to High Street gossip. And there was plenty to gossip about because at one time, not so very long ago, nearly everyone in the village worked nearby, on the land or in the shop. It was a shared workplace and a common way of life. The village never had a 'community centre'. The village *was* the community, in all its commonality and glorious Chaucerian diversity.

It was the centre of life for another perfectly straightforward reason. It was often difficult to get to anywhere else. Village girls married village boys, and families traced their lineage back to ancient days. The writer, Derek Sheffield, dates the decline of his village community to the day the first motorized bus arrived. Sixty years later, no one worked there any more except the vicar, the publican and a couple of tradespeople. From the centre of the universe to the dormitory of the town: that is the story of rural life during the past half-century.

This village is in Kent, in Wealden country, west of the Medway. Here the natives are known as Kentish Men, to emphasize their distinct identity from their

'The Garden of England': the cowled roof of the oast
looms above the ripening apples.

compatriots east of the river who are Men of Kent. Of course, you are neither until you have lived there for a very long time. Kentish Men live in a universe of fruit orchards and hop yards, whose produce is destined for London brewers and marketplaces. East of the Medway is a more patchwork landscape of crops and small, hedged fields with the great, green whalebacks of the Downs rolling eastward to the sea. Both tribes are gently self-deprecating about one another. One well-known expression is: 'Kentish born and Kentish bred. Strong in arm and weak in head.'

The Revd John Green, vicar of a rural parish in west Kent, sums up the essence of the villager's attitude to life:

> He was nearly always connected to the land in some way. A typical villager was slow to speak and thought first about what he was going to say. He had a philosophical outlook on the things that mattered to him – on his work, his garden and family life, as well as on life in general. He had an insatiable interest in everybody else in the village. This expressed itself in garden fence gossip, of course, but he would be genuinely concerned if someone was ill or unhappy. You rejoiced with them and mourned with them, and comment was usually kindly rather than too critical. You somehow found more life going on when everyone was on foot rather than in a motor car.

What sealed the community was friendship. To Brian 'Binky' Rogers, friendship is the essence of country life: 'Seeing people you've worked with for fifty years. I go there now and it's "Hello, Bink, how are you, Bink?" It's nice to be known, you know, and it all comes from working there.' Did the BBC series *The Darling Buds of May* get it right, then? 'The image wasn't too far from the truth. But Pop Larkin was too obviously a wide-boy to be a typical farmer, and though the rural scenes were convincing, we weren't quite as rural as *that!*'

While every village is physically different (you only have to look at the church, or the infinite variations on the village inn), in another sense they are all akin. Ambridge, the village in radio's *The Archers,* may have an identifiable geographical location, but it is really Everyvillage, the stage of rural living, its props the commonplace details of daily life. Hence I need not identify Derek Sheffield's village of forty years ago – for those with country memories, it might well be theirs:

Our High Street had two bakers, a cobbler-cum-saddler, there was still a black-smith's forge, and the church, a primary school and the Post Office. Oddly enough, it was the forge that survived – it turned into a garage. Our publican was a kind of uncrowned king: his palace faced a little green, and not far away we had three duck ponds, full of frog spawn in the spring. But to me, as a child, the real wonderland was The Shop. It was run by an elderly man and his wife, who never seemed to stop bickering. There were groceries to the right of the door, real groceries, not supermarket packages. I remember sides of bacon hanging up, and stacks of round cheeses, and tins of broken biscuits. Beyond the hams there were essential things like tins of paraffin, mousetraps, clothes pegs and sacks of corn, where the old dears would park themselves when they gathered there on Saturday morning. To the left was the haberdashery, with huge rolls of brightly-coloured material overlooking a polished mahogany counter. An inlaid brass rule had been worn smooth by all the cloth being unrolled, thumped over, thumped back again and put away. My grandfather told me there used to be thick sawdust all over the plank floor – to mop up the blood when they cut their fingers on the bacon slicer, Grandad said.

It's funny what sticks in your mind from childhood. Sweets, of course – for the local writer, Joan Kent, 'stickjaw toffee and sherbet dabs and big round gobstop-pers which you kept taking out to see what colour they'd turned'. They still make gobstoppers, of course, but not nearly so big and gobstopping. Derek Sheffield remembers a riding boot in the shop window – 'not a pair, just a single boot'. And in Joan's spit-and-sawdust pub there were always 'three pickled eggs floating in vinegar. We called them Faith, Hope and Charity, and everyone reckoned they'd been there for years.'

In this part of Kent, many villages were surrounded by orchards so that each spring the roofs of the houses seemed to float on a sea of pink and white blossom. Kent is, of course, 'the Garden of England' – a fruit garden, of cherry orchards and apple orchards, of strawberry acres and hop yards. Dickensians may recall Mr Jingle's view on this subject in *Pickwick Papers*: 'Kent, sir – everybody knows Kent

OVERLEAF A Kent apple orchard in blossom, the trees rooted in a wash of buttercups and other wild flowers.

– apples, cherries, hops and women.' I had often wondered about the 'women'. But it is, of course, the women who traditionally pick the cherries and hops and apples. Picking ripe cherries, without bruising or dropping them, needs a certain dexterity and finesse, and on the whole women are better at it than men. As for hops, they were picked by female cockneys and gypsies. Some men thought the work beneath them.

The onset of spring was sudden and overwhelming – the whole country seemed to burst into bloom, from the lilac trees in the cottage gardens to the banks carpeted with primroses, celandines and lady's smocks, which some called 'milk-maids'. Children knew the names of the wild flowers, partly because they picked them on the way to school and kept them in jam jars on their desks. Clive Baxter, a fruit-grower, remembers those scented springs.

> **The scent of apple and plum blossom in the spring can be overpowering. You took your children there to experience it. Cherry, too, sometimes, but though pear blossom looks lovely, the smell isn't half so sweet. The impact of orchards is all the greater because you've only just come out of winter, and the leaves aren't yet out. One moment you've got what seems to be deep winter, then suddenly there's this splash of white and pink all round the village.**

It was hardly surprising that May Day was a flower festival, a celebration of renewal – the sap rising in the branches of the fruit trees and the chestnut coppices, the sudden dam-burst of nature's pent-up energy. The village May Queen – the prettiest, or the wittiest, or merely the most popular girl – became a kind of flower herself as she was led in procession, in shimmering white, by her maids, all garlanded with flowers, and by a pair of little pageboys dressed in blue. It was perhaps in conscious mockery of all this floral pomp that the procession was sometimes accompanied by a village naughty boy, dressed up as a jester in cap and bells. In some villages, the children wore fancy dress, based on nursery rhyme characters – Old King Cole, Miss Muffet and her Spider, Simple Simon and so on. After the procession there were races, and of course maypole dancing, each child holding a coloured streamer which wound and unwound as they skipped in and out and around to the tune of a pianola or an old 78 r.p.m. gramo-phone record: 'Come lasses and lads, get leave of your dad, and weave the maypole high.'

Maypole dancing at the May Fair in Offham, 1966.

Elaborate yet intimate, such May Days were only possible in a close community. They were usually the joint production of school and church. 'We were aware of the pagan associations,' recalls Derek Sheffield. 'My grandmother told me it was all to do with the regeneration of life. When I was very young, young men and women would stay out until late, and return with blossom and greenery, looking a bit wan.' As Joan Kent puts it: 'You shed your chrysalis of winter clothing like a cabbage white butterfly. Among the tea parties and races and tugs-o'-war, I remember there was a baby show. The fattest baby always won it – it was like measuring up baby pigs. Never mind if they caught bronchitis.' It was, among other things, a festival of superstition. You did not get married in May, unless you had to. And you weren't supposed to wash any blankets either, for 'wash a blanket in May, washes a loved one away'.

ABOVE A croaking chorus of frogs from a village pond.
RIGHT The coppice woodland of Kent, an ideal habitat for the nightingale.

The dark clouds of 1939–45 washed away the English May Day. Some villages revived the tradition afterwards, but veterans of pre-war May Days believe that they never regained the same close and carefree spirit. But in recent years, Derek Sheffield has noticed a return in some villages of a wavelet of nostalgia, or perhaps a sense of something vital lost – 'The children are dancing round the maypoles again. It's definitely coming back, you know.'

Late spring was a time for bird-scaring, for the first cricket matches and for messing about in ponds. 'Water always attracts children, doesn't it? I think I'd fallen into every pond in the village by the time I was ten.' To Derek, ponds were things to slide on in winter, and for playing around on the way to and from school. 'You'd also lie in the grass with the sun on your back watching the water boatmen, the tadpoles and the newts. Children no longer seem to play around ponds the way we did. These days everybody collects their children from school, and so a slice of childhood has gone.'

Joan Kent's pond had an overhanging branch, which they would clamber along and lower jam jars on a string. 'It had plenty of frogs, and crested newts too, which looked like prehistoric monsters through the glass. I always tried to make friends with the frogs in case one of them turned into a prince. They never did, of course, just as you never found the end of a rainbow, let alone a crock of gold under it.'

Living in close proximity to nature turned some children into naturalists without really trying. They were always doing things that some modern, urban-living 'greens' would disapprove of. Ted Coleman, the local naturalist, remembers watching enthralled as a pair of kingfishers once took up residence in a sand pit used by nesting sand martins. 'We used to go there to steal their eggs, I'm afraid, putting our arm down their burrows, groping for the nest. Most village boys went through an egg-collecting phase then. It was a fashion, like most children's activities. You'd take an intense interest in something for about six weeks, then grow bored and do something else.'

John Green's love of the countryside and its wildlife 'started as soon as I was old enough to notice things. My knowledge grew almost unconsciously, really. My parents were moderately interested in flora and fauna, and I had an uncle who was an entomologist. He used to show me his insect cabinets and books, and soon got me involved in collecting, which increased my knowledge. Though I've long since ceased collecting, I've been able to recognize all sorts of specimens because of it. We were also lucky in having a large rectory garden with a paddock at the back, a wonderful environment to grow up in and enjoy.'

Not that every bird or insect was as welcome as the swifts returning to the church tower, or the nightingales to the chestnut wood. Before blossom time, orchard owners had a running battle with the bud-hungry bullfinches and, later on when the fruit was turning red, with the invading hordes of blackbirds and starlings. Ted Coleman remembers the bird-scarers' tents beneath the trees, the regular patrols, often armed with a shotgun: 'It was almost like a war going on.' Bird-scaring was often a farm child's weekend job, especially at Easter when the labourers were given time off to dig their potatoes. One way to scare the birds was to wave a rattle or bang an old dustbin lid at random moments. Another was to roar

PREVIOUS PAGES A cricket match in progress
on the village green at Bearsted, near Maidstone,
in 1957.

The bullfinch, colourful marauder of fruit tree buds.

around the orchards on an old motor bike, though that method isn't popular with neighbours first thing in the morning. Nowadays, most fruit-growers use a gas-operated gun. Joan Kent used to rehearse the school play with her sister.

> I learned a lot of Shakespeare while scaring the birds. I remember one year we did *The Merchant of Venice*. I'd stand waving an enormous wooden rattle, while Nora, who was playing Portia, went to the other side of the orchard. 'The quality of mercy is not strained …' she'd bellow, and I'd yell back, 'I can't hear you.' Then she'd shout her lines again, louder still, and I'd respond with Shylock: 'My deeds upon my head! I crave the law.'

Early summer saw the village green in use as a cricket pitch. The poet Edmund Blunden once remarked that cricketing in Kent came as naturally to him as the air he breathed. 'Cricket is summer, and summer is cricket.' It was not necessarily very good cricket, in terms of batting averages or the effectiveness of the bowling. Peter Tipples' village was more renowned for its cricketing teas than its matches. 'That might have been the reason we were so popular, the wives coming out with sandwiches and cakes, fresh strawberries and cherries.' Village cricket personifies the English summer: the cricketing whites, the crack of the willow bat and the staccato patter of applause, the shading elms, the church steeple smiling over the English at play, and the sweet, green summer haze.

The first trees to ripen fruit were the cherries, and cherry-picking made June a busy month in many villages. On Rogation Sunday there was often a kind of orchard ritual, in which John Green would ask God's blessing on the trees and on the labours of those working there. 'It's part of the role of the church in the countryside, proclaiming God's part in our daily living and our daily food.' Cherry trees are tall, and the picking is ladder-work. Men placed the ladders, and women plucked nimbly among the branches and leaves, bearing a wicker basket hooked on to a stave. Cherries were a poor crop for the nervous, and not only for fear of heights or dropping the fruit. A late frost, or a severe thunderstorm, or a swarm of bullfinches, could ruin the entire crop. Unseasonal frosts split open the flesh, so that the cherries would 'seem to laugh at you' through smile-shaped cracks. But a failed crop was no joke for the farmer when times were already hard. When a tremendous hailstorm destroyed Peter Tipples' fruit, and made his hop poles look 'as though someone had fired a twelve-bore at them', he spent much of his unexpected spare time that summer playing cricket. 'It was the only thing that kept me sane.'

After the cherries came the plums, and then the apples and pears, and lastly there were the potatoes to dig. 'The seasons seemed to last longer then.' Much of the fruit went straight to Covent Garden on the evening train. Ted Coleman remembers the queue of carts at the goods yard, loaded high with cherry baskets, 'each carefully sealed with blue paper, held down by withies of hazel, bent crossways like a hot-cross bun'. Derek Sheffield's grandfather used to trade with a local smallholder, who would arrive at the end of the day with his lorry. 'He and Grandad would go into a corner, and there'd be a lot of spitting on hands and hand-shakes, and pound notes were exchanged. Grandad would spin it out, saying how he'd flogged himself to the bone and what a terrible job it had been, but it was us, lying on the lawn exhausted, that had done all the work.'

A generation ago, nearly every farm in the Kentish Weald contained orchards, full of big, standard apple trees: Bramleys, Worcesters, Cox's, and other, less familiar ones, like the Gladstone, which didn't compare with the others in taste but ripened a whole week earlier, so for just that long it tasted delicious. Many farmers

Cherry-picking on tall ladders, traditionally a job for women.

still grow fruit, and probably always will – every Wealden farmer will tell you that English fruit in general, and Kentish in particular, is the most delicious in the world, thanks to our slow-ripening weather. But the acreage is smaller than it was, and the lovely but awkward old trees are steadily being replaced by younger, bushier growth in which the fruit can be picked *sans* ladder at chest height. The picking season, too, has shrunk, from several weeks to a few days, and with it much of the party atmosphere. It no longer involves the villagers, at least not to the same extent as it did.

There are other problems. Fruit-picking is labour-intensive, and is not as profitable as it used to be. And, because throughout the European Union most orchard fruit is now in surplus, farmers are being paid £1800 an acre (0.4 hectares) to grub up their trees. Supermarkets have added their pennyworth of woe by stocking European varieties which are cheaper than home-grown produce although – arguably – inferior in flavour. Clive Baxter, whose family has grown fruit for generations (and his orchards stand on the site of a Roman vineyard) is sad about the premature loss of so many beautiful orchards.

> There's terrific competition from the EU now, where English farmers are up against France and Italy, where fruit-growing is easier. I also think our customers are losing any sense of seasonality. You can buy strawberries at Christmas time now, which I think is a pity. There are such quantities of apples in the supermarkets all year round that people forget that if they buy Bramleys in spring they are probably from last year's crop. Maybe some people don't ask themselves where the fruit comes from. It's just something in a shop. Mind you, I think there's some move to bring back freshness and flavour into fruit. People are more willing to pay that bit extra for something that not only looks good but tastes better. Even our competitors seem to realize this – for example, the so-called Golden Delicious apple, which doesn't taste of anything much, is going out of fashion. So long as people demand quality, there's hope for fruit-growing in Kent.

While the last of the cherries were being picked, and the sheep and chickens were being turned out of the apple and pear orchards (for fear the sheep should upset the ladders), the next great event of the season was beginning: the annual exodus from the East End to the hop yards of Kent. The farmer would collect them from the station, whole families, some with babies in prams and young children new to the sights and sounds of the country, and perhaps joined by gypsies and gangs of often Irish itinerants who used to roam the pre-war countryside in search of work. It was the kind of popular working holiday made possible only when an industrial cityscape out of Dickens' *Hard Times* lay close to one of L.P. Hartley's rural idylls. Townie and villager met each other with mutual incomprehension. The hop-pickers lived in camps, close to the yards. Ernie Davis, a regular hopper in the 1950s, remembers their huts as 'very basic – corrugated iron with a wooden floor and straw-stuffed pillows and palliasses to sleep on, which made you itch like hell. Outside every hut there was a brick fireplace, what you'd call a barbecue now, with a pot over the top to cook on, usually something out of an old oven. There was a cookhouse, which we used when it rained, but mostly people cooked outside, like a camp fire.'

The hop gardens themselves were bounded off with gates and fences. Another regular, Joan Cullip, recalls:

There was a wonderful atmosphere in the hop yard – very friendly, and of course a lot of us knew one another – we were nearly all from the East End. Everything that happened to you seemed funny. The pole-pullers were always flirting with the girls, and in the evening the older ones would start up with sentimental songs – 'There's an old mill by the stream, Nelly Dean', 'She's my lady love' – as well as some special hopping songs like 'When you go down hopping'. The singing mingled with the brew-ups of tea, and woodsmoke and cooking pots, and the scent of the meadows – it smelled a lot better than smoke in London, I can tell you.

My family used to do 'the complete farm', all summer long from May to September. First there was the hop-training, then the strawberries and bringing in the hay, then hop-picking, and after that it was into the orchards to pick the apples. Sometimes we even stayed on for the Brussels sprouts. The farm was our home for half the year. My mum really became a country yokel. She came down here the first time when she was nineteen, and I buried her here when she died, aged eighty-one. Someone said she'd enjoy the view from the cemetery, and I didn't realize what he meant at first: it overlooked the farm she'd worked on most of her life. She just loved Kent.

Mind you, the local villagers always looked down on us. Some kids stared and mimicked us when we walked down the street. A few even threw stones, and there was the odd punch-up. We were supposed to be noisy, vulgar and dirty, and we got accused if anything went missing. The shops put wire-netting over the counters, but there were ways and means. I think the older villagers miss the hop-pickers now, because we always treated the old boys in the pub, and made things a bit more lively.

Peter Tipples gives a glimpse of what they thought about all this from the other side of the hop yard wall.

Our village was full of pubs – nine or ten of them – and, you might think, how can they possibly drink that much? Well, we didn't, it was the Londoners that kept them in business. They'd come in by the hundred on payday in the hop gardens,

PREVIOUS PAGES East End families working in the hop yard.
ABOVE A hop-pickers' encampment near Goudhurst, Kent, in 1949.
Note the bundles of faggots, cut from local woods and used as
campfire fuel.

and have a marvellous time, laughing and singing. But they weren't so cheerful
getting back, because they weren't used to the dark country lanes, you know.
That was when we'd play tricks on them, hiding and making ghost noises. Once I
made a turnip lantern and put it up on a gate with a sheet round it and, do you
know, they wouldn't go past it, they made a big detour to get back. Another time
we had a guy jump down in an old parachute on a piece of elastic. Whooo! It
frightened the hell out of them, though he banged his head on a branch when he
bounced back up. It was no reflection on them. I'm sure I'd have felt the same on
London streets at night.

The one thing no one seems to have enjoyed was actual hop-picking. The hops are, of course, flowers, and had to be carefully separated from the prickly 'bine' and its festoons of leaves. There was a technique which you learned by experience, pulling down the bine and laying it across the hop bin with one hand, and stripping it of hops with the other. Soon your hands would be black with hop juice. Joan Cullip remembers: 'It was pick, pick, pick, and you could never get your hands clean afterwards. The only thing that got it off was paraffin, and then everything tasted of paraffin as you ate your tea.' Ted Coleman adds: 'It was a terrible job, getting stained and scratched by the prickles. I always tried to get out of it. Unfortunately, the season coincided with the school holidays, and I was expected to earn something towards the cost of my school uniform.' As for Ernie Davis: 'I never picked a single hop. I was always next door, scrumping apples or messing about.'

The hopping holidays stopped suddenly, at the end of the 1950s. Ernie remembers 'a lot of talk about machines replacing hand-pickers, but few of us thought they ever would. But they did, and so quickly, too.' Thanks to new, low-climbing hop varieties, and devices that systematically strip the vines and sift out the debris, Ernie's farm, which once employed 2000 pickers, now gets by with only 30, mainly students. By 1980, the old hop-pickers' huts had all gone. It was the end of an era. And many of the oast-houses – those wonderful hop-drying barns with their characteristically bent chimney cowls – 'to keep the weather out' – those too are falling out of use. Many have become homes or offices, or some other borrowing, in which the last link with hop yards is the home brew in the cupboard under the stairs. Vernon Millen used to enjoy his seasonal job as the local hop-drier, with the sacks of fresh hops and the big, glowing kilns and the aroma of the roasting hops. 'The smell and heat of the oast could make you feel very sleepy, if you weren't careful. And a very nice sleep it was, too.' His oast is now the country home of some City stockbroker.

On most farms today there is only one harvest – a brief mechanical cropping conducted by the man inside the combine harvester. In the old days it could last weeks, and around the Kentish village there would be several harvests all in a row – cherries, hay, apples, hops and corn. Memories are already fading of the pre-industrial harvest when women reapers in long skirts and shawls tied the sheaves with plaited straw. But many still remember the hay cocks drying in the sun before being pitched on to carts and taken to the stack. The haystack provided another rich opportunity for fun and games, as Derek Sheffield recalls.

You don't see real haystacks now. They were wonderful to look at, like little cottages, with their thatched tops full of mice and rats. The harvest was a very busy time, people sometimes working until late in the night by firelight, sweating and fuming, and drinking all the beer the farmer could provide. Us lads wouldn't help matters by tunnelling into the haystacks, coming up in the middle, and lying in the sun on top to watch the world go by, with *The Beano* or *Dandy,* and a bottle of pop.

When they weren't dreaming on haystacks, many schoolboys were 'scrumping' fruit from the orchards. With fruit trees so close, it was all too easy to regard them as a kind of free-for-all village garden, despite the fences and warning notices. The raiding parties of Derek Sheffield and his friends attracted the attention of the local bobby:

This particular constable was the bane of our lives. I remember he lay in wait for us once, one Saturday afternoon, and suddenly appeared from behind a tree. We all ran like billy-o out of the orchard and across the potato fields, but unfortunately he recognized one of us and went round to his parents. We all ended up in Bromley Magistrates' Court, but because the case involved only half a pound of cherries the magistrate kicked it out. I heard later that the constable wasn't above a bit of scrumping himself. Someone saw him riding home on his bike after his stint in the orchard with cherry juice dripping out of his carrier bag!

The old mixed farms of The Weald were 'highly needing in labour', as Peter Tipples puts it. Today, though, farms are being forced to produce as cheaply as possible, without high labour costs. Peter regrets the passing of the old-style farm and its close relations with the village.

Today, most farms are switching to arable, cereal-growing, because, so long as you have the acreage, that's where the money is. As one big farmer told me, 'I'll grow anything that I can put through a combine harvester.' We still keep a few sheep, but we're hanging on by our fingernails there. Once nearly all of the cottages in our village were rented by farm-workers. I doubt whether there are more than four of them so occupied now. Our farm has doubled in size but from twelve farm-workers we're down to two, plus some part-time help during the picking. As for the small 50-acre [20-hectare] farmer who used to grow apples and hops, and keep a few pigs, he just isn't making ends meet any more. He'll be forced to sell his land, and it'll be turned into a paddock for some city gent's daughter's pony.

In the woods, though, certain ancient and, one might have supposed, long-lost crafts are still practised. On still days in late autumn you may spy a trickle of blue-grey smoke rising above the chestnut wood on the hilltop above the village. Ray Wheeler, the wood-reeve, is at work, making charcoal for garden barbecues. He explains what he does:

> We use big metal kilns to produce the charcoal, the usual method hereabouts these past fifty years. They act like a giant wood-burning stove: you load them up

A charcoal-burner at work in a Kentish wood, August 1951.
The secret was to maintain a slow, steady fire, which the burner
is damping down with a bucket of water.

with sections of wood, set them alight and control the draught in the same way as you would a stove, so that you burn some of the wood but turn the rest to charcoal. We got into charcoal-burning because the old market for coppice wood collapsed when the local pulp-mill shut down – they used to take 120 000 tons [122 000 tonnes] of wood a year. Charcoal-burning had all but died out in England, but suddenly there's a demand for it for barbecue stoves. It's mad that most of our barbecue charcoal is imported – they are even planting eucalyptus trees in the tropics just to produce it – when we've got thousands of acres of neglected coppice woodland here which is perfect for charcoal. After all, that's what a lot of these woods did, before coal and coke became widely available.

To produce a regular supply of charcoal, you've got to get the wood into production again, cutting it over on a regular cycle so you've always got trees at the right stage of growth. I think I'm one of the last wood-reeves in the country – certainly the only one in our phone book. It's a name that went with the coppice trade; it means the man in charge of the wood, literally the 'mayor' of the wood. Both my father and grandfather were wood-reeves, and I hope my son will be following in our footsteps. Mind you, he might be the last, the way the wood trade is going. In the old days the wood-reeve was a very responsible job, because wood was a basic commodity for everything from building repair to hedging binders, firewood and garden tools. If you look at the old estate records, you'll see they didn't waste a thing. Even the brush from the tops was made into faggots for the bakers' ovens or for the hop-pickers' fires.

The main kind of commercial coppice wood in Kent is sweet chestnut, those shady trees with furrowed bark and long, dark green serrated leaves. It is not a native tree, though it has been grown in Britain since Roman times, and one of the country's oldest living trees is, in fact, a sweet chestnut. In Britain's cool climate it likes, as Ray put it, 'a bank where the sun can drop in when it shines'. In the older woods of Kent, chestnut grows happily with trees like hazel, hornbeam and oak, often above carpets of bluebells in May. The great virtue of the chestnut is the speed at which it springs back after a cutting.

We cut ours in winter, at about fourteen years of growth. Chestnut grows so fast that by the end of the following summer the regrowth is already taller than me. My job is to look after the coppice, mark out the wood sale areas and organize general care and maintenance, planting in the gaps, things like that. Some of these woods have been cut over for two or three hundred years, as you can tell by the size of the stocks (the base of the bush), 6 or 7 feet [2 metres] across. The cut wood is still used for a variety of purposes. Palings for fences is the main one, but some will be sold for tree stakes. One of the really big local markets was for hop poles – I remember one buyer telling me he needed 18 000 hop poles that year – but now they string the hops up on wires. Another lost trade was bark for the tanning factories. I remember my father 'flawling the oak', that is stripping the bark with a special metal tool. He used to do it in the early spring, when the wood was getting sappy and the bark came away easily. I think there's only one person left in this country that still sells bark. Even twenty years ago, we'd have had forty prospective buyers at our wood sales, whereas we'd be lucky now to have ten.

As the year nears its darkened end and the village prepares for Christmas, we might contemplate the changes that have swept over it, in most of our lifetimes. It has seen the end of isolation, and the old interdependent way of life. The nature of the farm, the basic unit of the Kentish countryside, has changed utterly (though perhaps not irrevocably): it is less of a working community now, and more of a work space. And, of all counties, it is Kent that has to contend most with becoming a kind of marshalling yard for Europe, a place to rush through by car or fast train, a green promontory between London and France. To Ted Coleman, 'Kent is still the Garden of England, but it's fast becoming the Motorway of Europe too, with the Channel Tunnel and the rail link.' The relaxed way of life, the sense that things will never change fundamentally, that next year the hop-pickers will be back, that the carts will once again be queuing at the station with their loads of fruit, is passing. Perhaps many would be bored by it all now. But the older people of the village miss it, although many find it is possible to blend nostalgia with the countryman's innate sense of philosophy. Like the Revd John Green:

I enjoyed being able to wander around on my own, without fear of traffic or any other danger. I can remember farmers driving their sheep for miles along the Downs and lanes without having to worry about cars and lorries. I suppose my memories are centred round a leisurely country life in a largish house and garden, and a village where everyone knew you and you knew everybody. I think people had more time then, they didn't feel rushed all the time, constantly

The familiar and hopefully enduring landmarks
of a village in 'the Garden of England':
orchards and oasts at Newington in the 1950s.

looking at their watches. I think that feeling is rather lost nowadays, and life has become much noisier. What has worried me since the war was whether Kent would lose its character. I believe it hasn't, in spite of the motorways and all the cars and people going to and fro to the Continent. In many parts, it's still the Garden of England, the best county of all.

Many of the symbols of village life, the outward signs – the church bells, the thatched cottages and terraces of mismatched architectural styles, the pond by the green and the wood on the hill – still remain, as pleasurable to roam among as ever. Perhaps the danger to some villages is not so much physical destruction as well-meaning over-elaboration: the cloying quaintness of the coach lamps and horse brasses and those little stone 'mushrooms' whose original function is virtually forgotten. Villages should look lived in, not just slept in, and God defend them from becoming 'open-air museums'. Nostalgia for the past does not exclude vitality in the present nor optimism for the future. But socially, if not physically, some villages have been transformed as radically as in the distant days when Hengist and Horsa drove the Ancient Britons from Kent and pastured their cattle in the empty towns. Derek Sheffield has seen it happen in his lifetime.

I sometimes walk through the churchyard now and see my whole life lying there. Everyone I grew up with is there. To me, what makes a place a happy one is the people who lived there; they were wonderful people, and I feel privileged that I knew them, and that I lived in their time.

One of my most vivid memories is of a Spitfire doing a victory roll in the blue sky over a cornfield, some time in 1943. I watched this beautiful machine turning so gracefully in the air, and I resolved that one day I was going to do that, in the same piece of sky over the village where I was brought up. And I did, too, twenty years later, not in a Spitfire, of course, but in a Mark 21 Chipmunk. I performed a big barrel roll over Eighteen Acres Field, and – and this still chokes me when I talk about it – I looked up at the village from upside down, and then suddenly I realized that every single person I'd ever known or loved there had gone. Even our house had gone. Here I was, showing off, showing what I could do, and I was playing to an empty theatre. There was no one left.

POSTCARD

— Chapter Two —

Beside the Sea

THE CORNISH COAST

MANY OF US still cherish that wonderful childhood sense of eager anticipation when our holiday train slipped into Padstow or Penzance, or when we crossed the Tamar and first caught sight of the sea. Cornwall has always seemed a land apart. Even now, when it lies within a weekend's reach of Birmingham and London, the Cornish coast continues to promise adventure – fishing trips and surf rides, rock pools and coves to explore, and cream teas in whitewashed cottages. But perhaps most of us went home without learning much about the people who live and work in these enchanted places.

Some of the fishing villages, like Polperro or Mousehole (pronounced *Mouz*-el), look so impossibly quaint that it is hard to imagine them as workplaces: they seem as if they were designed to delight the incomer. But though they perform for tourists, most of these villages are workplaces still. Their prettiness is not so much the product of design as of geology. They cluster in the sheltered pockets of a wild coast with few large, natural harbours, and their stone- and slate-built houses rise, often steeply, above the quay, with cobbled streets winding down to the boats.

Harlyn Bay. To the summer visitor the stereotype
beach scene appears not to have changed.

Cornish fishing is usually a family business, a cottage industry. The fish are – or, at least, were – plentiful in these Atlantic-warmed waters, but the traditional fishing boat was small, and was owned by its skipper. Fishing was not a livelihood that earned a fortune, but it bred shrewd, hardy, laid-back men and self-reliant communities, a shared way of life beside the sea. Behind the tea shops and the smugglers' inns, they continue to land their catch of white fish or mackerel and support a variety of jobs in the village. Whether there will be a future for the small boats after the big Spanish trawlers move in in 1996 remains to be seen. It is an anxious time in the fishing trade. And there is more than the loss of livelihoods at stake. The survival of the independent spirit of old Cornwall may depend on the outcome of discussions between anonymous civil servants in far-away cities.

Portscatho is one of many small communities that cluster around every cove and natural harbour on that jagged, treacherous stretch of coast between Fowey and Falmouth. Civic pride is obvious in the neat, whitewashed cottages arrayed in tiers above the harbour and the well-kept gardens and streets. But, outside the busy tourist season, it is a quieter, emptier place than it was in its fishing heyday, fifty years ago. Many of the houses are now second homes, and where there were once fifty fishing boats drawn up on the beach there are now only five. Hilary Thompson, whose family has lived here for generations, remembers the old sense of bustle on the harbour-front.

You'd see many stores and fish-sheds by the quayside, some once used as pilchard cellars, but now dark places housing nets, oars and other gear. There would be stacks of crab pots, and old nets – real fibre nets, not monofilament ones – drying on the harbour chains. The old nets were made of natural hemp, dipped in water in which oak bark had been soaked to preserve them, so they had that lovely smell of oak. I miss the old smells of the village. At the harbour you'd have smelt fish very strongly. When the men came in with their catches, anything they didn't want they'd just chuck over the side. When they gutted the fish, the insides went over too. And they used to cut up scraps, usually of dog-fish, to bait the crab pots. It reeked of fish. In the spring you'd also smell tar, which was heated up at home to paint the boat's bottom, inside and out. The

A street scene at Bodinnick Ferry, a typical Cornish fishing village with steep, narrow streets and stuccoed cottages rising above the harbour.

fishermen were all dressed alike, in Guernsey sweaters and old baggy trousers, and old peaked caps with an oily blob on the crown. They used to go out fishing in the summer, and in winter make a living as best they could, collecting oysters in the Fal, or whatever labouring work they could find.

Janette Eathorne has spent most of her life in St Ives, on the north coast. Her house was one of a terrace of sixteen, all but three of which are now let to holiday-makers. She remembers it as a grand place to grow up.

Janette Eathorne as a small girl.

Everyone had a rowing boat, and when we weren't at school we'd be down on the beach from first thing in the morning to last thing at night, winter as well as summer. I remember the big, blue skies, and the lovely, warm sea and sand with so much room to run on. We went 'mullying' – that is catching small fish with cotton and hooks, using limpets as bait. We gave names to all the rock pools: there was Shark Pool, Poacher Pool, the Bathing Pool, and so on. After Christmas, we'd go round the houses asking for the Christmas trees, which we'd carry to the beach. We'd stick them in the sand and decorate them with seaweed, tinsel and anything else we could find.

In places like Portscatho and St Ives, boys were brought up to be fishermen, while also earning pocket-money doing farm work. They were at home in rowing boats from an early age, gaining a knowledge of the sea, of tides and currents and of the fishing grounds. To earn pocket-money, they also became apprentice farmers. Leslie Hicks, who was born in Polruan, was already working on small-holdings at the age of ten, milking and cleaning out the cow sheds. But most of his leisure time was spent in and around the sea.

We'd paddle with our shorts rolled up, and play games with stuff we'd combed on the beach. We didn't have many toys. But we'd make little boats out of crab shells, or shape bits of driftwood into a tug boat, and give them a mast with a paper sail. Then we'd have a competition to see which boat was fastest. We were learning the skills for when we got older. We also earned a few bob in summer rowing tourists round the harbour. We'd get the boats tied and cleaned up – the seagulls were always mucking up the seats, so the first thing we did was to clean them out with a rag, until the boat was spick and span, like a taxi driver would do. We learned at an early age how to row, and you'd be despised as an amateur if you lifted the paddles very far out of the water.

Like so many of their neighbours, the Hicks family owned a smallholding – hardly more than an allotment – on which they grew their own vegetables. They also sold some produce at the market. Their speciality was spring flowers, taking advantage of the mild, often frost-free winters and the early Cornish springs. This harvest took place between January and March, before the fishing season really got underway. For the rest of the year, the digging, potting and other tasks were done whenever they could be fitted in between fishing trips. A generation ago,

Daffodil-picking near Lamorna in about 1935, in one of
the many small fields along the coast cultivated by fishermen
and quarrymen to supplement their income.

these 'fishermen's acres' supplied the rest of the country with early potatoes and spring flowers. Daffodils and violets were especially in demand, and boxes of fresh flowers used to be taken on the local bus service to Penzance station, whence they were transported by rail to Covent Garden and to Birmingham. The violets were sold mainly in the Midlands, for Mother's Day. Nowadays, of course, early new potatoes are imported from Egypt and Cyprus, and few florists stock the once fashionable little bunches of scented violets. Most of the smallholdings have been abandoned and are reverting to nature. Once tended with such care, these pockets of cultivation are now given over to bramble and bracken.

Another winter job was making crab and lobster pots from the supple wands of willow, known as withies. David Chapple used to go up on to the moors after Christmas and cut his own wild withies from the scrub willows growing there. But others were obtained from little gardens of planted willow by one of the streams that run down the cliffs into the sea. These withies made the bars of the pot. The extra-supple ones needed for the binding were usually obtained from commercial beds in Somerset. Many of the Portscatho fishermen had little sheds where the pot-making was done.

> You'd bring the withies back and trim them up to make an even stand of rods. Then you work the mouth round with the Somerset withies and you tie them down to make the shape of an inkwell. After that, you work the withies round the binding, and once you've got the right shape and the right depth, you turn it over and bend in the withies to make the bottom. The last part is to bind the bottom in. For this you want some nice, thick withies because the pot's going to be sitting on the sea bed and it has to take all the chafe. We still make a few in that way, but more for show than anything else. The pots are all made of steel or plastic now, and they last maybe ten years, much longer than the old ones which used to fall to bits after a season or two. That's why we were always making new ones.

The pots may be plastic now, but many fishing villages still have a willow garden, a patch of willow pattern on the overgrown cliff. Look out for them – they all have a story to tell.

Fishing is the life-blood of the Cornish coast. For those who grew up there it was the natural way of life. Like his father and grandfather, Lewis Butters earned his living from the sea, and fishing provided most of the talk on the streets and in the taverns of Looe. After an apprenticeship as a boat-builder, Lewis joined his father on fishing trips and gradually took over the family business. In his grand-father's day, the main commercial fish was the pilchard, a shoal fish which was caught at night in seine nets – the big, purse-shaped nets that are towed by the trawler, scooping up the fish as they go. It is only in the relatively warm waters around Cornwall that large shoals of pilchards can be found in British waters. There were some huge catches in the early years of the century, the heyday of the Cornish pilchard fishery. On one memorable occasion, 13½ million pilchards were landed at Newlyn in a single day. That was exceptional, but Lewis Butters remembers some wonderful nights in the late 1940s when drift nets were haul-ing in up to 30 tons (30.5 tonnes) of pilchards a night.

> We had no echo-sounders or anything like that. When I started fishing, all we had on board was a compass. You relied on the sea-birds, especially the gannets, to tell you where the fish were. The old fishermen could prove nine times out of ten that the fish were moving against the wind. You could tell from the angle of the gannet's dive what he was fishing for. And you could smell the oil of the pilchards in the water. On a dead calm day you'd look for bubbles coming up from the fish. You watch them to see which direction the fish are moving in. Then you go up ahead of them and shoot your nets.

Most Cornish pilchards were exported to Italy, and so had to be preserved soon after the boats came in. Pilchard-pressing took place in the cool cellars of the houses near the harbour-front. Alternating layers of fish and salt were built up inside the cellar, with the smelly oil streaming out on to the cobblestones. After several weeks, the salt-preserved fish were washed and packed in barrels, with slits in the sides so the remaining oil could drain away. Traditionally, this was women's work – Lewis Butters' mother was one of them – and many took great pride in creating a rosette or 'flower' of pilchards at the top of the barrel before the lid was secured. The barrels were then taken to Falmouth to be loaded on to ships bound for the Mediterranean. The traditional way of pressing pilchards produced by far the tastiest fish. But it was both time-consuming and labour-intensive, and eventually, reluctantly, the Cornish were forced to adopt the quicker, cheaper, Spanish way of preserving the fish in brine, inside huge concrete tanks. Today, there is only one pilchard-pressing factory left, a kind of working museum. And the great nets that caught them are mostly gone. Hilary Thompson remembers being allowed to play on the mound of tangy rope, the last of the great seine nets of Portscatho, owned by her grandfather.

The big inshore fishery today is for mackerel. Newlyn is the main centre for mackerel in Britain, landing between one-third and one-half of the country's total catch. During summer, huge shoals of mackerel are netted by Cornish trawlers on the open sea. But in the autumn, the fish split up into much smaller shoals, and this gives the small-boat fisherman his chance to catch them with hook and line. This method, known as long-lining, uses twenty or more hooks strung out 'like washing on a line', and weighted to the sea bed by lead sinkers. A popular bait is made from coloured chicken feathers, attached to the line at intervals. The way in which they jig and flutter in calm water excites the mackerel so much that they charge at the line and hook themselves. The trick is to wind them up quickly

ABOVE Seine netting for pilchards. Huge catches were made
in the early years of the century.
RIGHT Newlyn, the main centre of the Cornish fishing industry.
Today these small boats compete with large Spanish trawlers.

but steadily so the fish do not have time to drop off. Long-lining for mackerel is a popular day out for tourists. David Chapple started long-lining after the Second World War, when food rationing meant that people were desperate for fresh fish.

When I started there were plenty of fish of every sort – mackerel, pilchard, pollack, bass. I'd hand-line for mackerel using feathers, which we'd pull through the shoal of fish. The faster you unhooked, the more fish you'd catch. I caught ½ ton [0.5 tonnes] of mackerel that way in one summer, and would sell 200 at a time. Everyone was after salt mackerel and pilchard for winter. We used to take fish to friends and exchange them for potatoes. One neighbour told me: 'You keep me in fish and I'll keep you in spuds!'

It isn't so easy to find fish today, despite the radios and echo-sounders on the cockpit of every boat.

In the early 1970s there were still a lot of mackerel, and things were going well for us. We were hand-lining, and everyone was buying new boats. Then suddenly the British trawlers were kicked out of Icelandic waters, and everyone turned to fishing Cornish mackerel. In five years, these trawlers from Yarmouth and Lowestoft ruined our market. They used to shoot purse seine nets round our shoals big enough to cover St Paul's Cathedral. It's much more difficult to make a living now. Life before was much more laid-back. At lunchtime, all the fishermen would congregate on one boat with their sandwiches and flasks. Now you see them fishing with sandwiches in their mouths. Twenty years ago, there were half-a-dozen species worth catching, and when everyone could diversify you weren't harming stocks. Now we're down to shellfish and mackerel – pollack, bass, sea bream, they're all gone. And it's getting more expensive. We bought a lorry to take our fish to Newlyn. Then we had to get a deep-freeze, which came off the back of an old truck. Now we're trying to get a permanent custom-built shed for a cold-room.

It is the familiar problem of too many boats chasing too few fish. Fifty years ago, most of the boats crowding every harbour were employed, one way or another, in commercial fishing. Today, the majority, at least in large harbours like Penzance, are more likely to be leisure boats for sailing, diving and sport fishing. And the greatest sport fishing of all is for sharks. The Cornish coast is where anglers converge in quest of big game – blue and mako sharks, congers and skate. Since the 1960s, taking parties shark-fishing has become an important summer activity for many Cornish skippers in centres, like Looe, where sharks gather in numbers. Their skill and experience are essential for a good day's fishing. Before sport fishing became popular, most fishermen regarded sharks as pests, not profit. They had multiplied during the war, when most big trawlers had been borrowed by the Navy for use as minesweepers. At first, shark-fishing was the hobby of a well-heeled few. Iven Chasten remembers a barrister from London catching no fewer than sixty-nine sharks in eight trips. In the 1950s and 60s, the excitement of shark-fishing attracted a much larger following; more and more boats were hired, 3–4000 sharks were caught each year, and most of them were killed. Over-fishing for the shark's main prey, mackerel, worsened the situation.

Cleaning and checking the nets on board the trawlers
at Looe harbour on market day.

The number of sharks fell abruptly, and by the early 1980s fewer than 200 sharks a year were being caught in Cornish waters. Rather belatedly shark fisheries realized that there is not an infinite supply of large fish. More sustainable methods of fishing were introduced and nowadays nearly every shark that is caught is released alive, apart from the really big ones, which can still be towed in, slung up and photographed, with the catcher standing proudly by. Recently, Iven Chasten was tagging and releasing sharks as part of a programme organized by the Shark Angling Club to assess their numbers. Iven reckons that the sharks have roughly doubled in number since the low point around 1980. But the once common sight of four or five blue sharks circling your boat is a rare experience today. The main threat to sharks now comes not from sport angling, but from commercial fishing boats using long nets that kill every fish they catch.

Shark-fishing is for the leisured few who yearn to pit their skill and strength against the largest and most agile fish in the sea. For the rest of us, there is always the eternal lure of beachcombing and the miniature, weed-hung world of the rock pool. Gillian Matthews remembers the delights of beachcombing fifty years ago, before tar balls and litter had begun to foul the coves.

I'd go with my father with a sack to collect driftwood. In those days, the wood was pretty clean and we'd use it as firewood. One thing we always used to look for were the green or white glass balls that the fishermen used to float their nets. Occasionally we'd find a blue or an orange one, which was extra special and sought-after. I remember coming across a giant fish, about 6 feet [2 metres] long – it was probably a tunny. Once I discovered a pith helmet. But the most exciting thing was a bottle with a message inside! I think it was genuine. It said, in French, 'My boat is in peril at the mouth of the Loire.' I wonder what happened to it, and whether he was rescued.

We also used to explore the rock pools with shrimping nets. One of my school teachers used to take us on nature outings. I remember once collecting from the rock pools on a rising tide and, while we were eagerly searching the pools, the tide crept over our school books and we turned round to see them floating out to sea!

Posing proudly for the camera: a scene from the shark-fishing heyday of the 1950s.

The beaches, too, had their treasures. Gillian used to go down to the strand at low tide to find razor shells for supper. Catching them demanded great cunning.

Razor shells burrow very fast in the sand, so fast they're almost impossible to dig up. What we used to do was look for the slit marks they make on the wet sand, like little keyholes. You take some salt, and pour it into this little groove, the entrance to the razor shell's burrow. Then you wait patiently, not moving. If it works, after a minute or so, up comes the razor shell and then, when it's about two-thirds out, you grab it. But if you're too quick, the shell will slip through your fingers and dive back down again. In those days we used to eat all sorts of things gathered from the beach – prawns, mussels, limpets. We don't now, of course.

A more serious form of beachcombing was 'wrecking' – not in the *Jamaica Inn* tradition of luring ships on to the rocks and then looting them, but in the harmless sense of picking up drifting beams, planks and other useful material from deck cargoes washed overboard in heavy seas. Harmless – but, strictly speaking, illegal. Such harvests of the sea were supposed to be reported to the coastguard or customs official, but there was an unwritten rule that anything that could be pulled above the high-water mark was yours. Hilary Thompson remembered one occasion when men were bringing in deck timber on their shoulders to hide away in sheds and barns. Suddenly, the customs man appeared on his motor bike.

'He asked my father whether he'd seen any signs of the timber. Quick as a flash, my father said, "Oh, I think it has come ashore at Pendower," on the far side of the bay, so the man thanked him and roared off on his bike – seconds before the men carrying the next load of wood appeared round the corner.'

Growing up in such surroundings, learning about the currents and the tides and the fickle ways of fish, natural history was a way of life for many. Gillian Matthews learned the names of the wild flowers through a competition organized by her school.

One of my teachers used to make a very thorough collection of local wild flowers – I think there were about 400 different species – which all the girls, from the youngest to the Sixth Form, had to try to name. I think all my contemporaries at school acquired a good knowledge of natural history thanks to her. I loved the little pink rest-harrow, partly because its name is so attractive, and the beautiful sheep's-bit, so piercingly blue. A botanist staying at my parents' guest house showed me some wild onions here at Portscatho, and the rare galingale, *Cyperus longus,* in a marsh nearby. One of the things that most excited me then was walking along the cliff path one evening and finding glow-worms.

I used to take a rowing dinghy on to the river on a dark, warm summer night and, if the conditions were right, you'd get a whirlpool of phosphorescence where we'd disturbed the water, and then see the drips of water falling from the oars, like diamonds. I used to love this. We'd throw pebbles in the water and watch the explosion of light caused by the scattering of the glowing micro-scopic life. Later I'd collect things from rock pools to look at the next day, and sometimes in the dark you'd see shooting across the container a little bright spark, some little shrimp or other animal shining with phosphorescent light. There was also a kind of worm covered in phosphorescent slime, and you could rub your hands with it and emerge as a sort of phosphorescent monster!

Ray Dennis' early love of rock pools led him to take up diving, exploring the wonderful gardens of anemones and differently coloured seaweeds that massed around the headlands and on the many wrecks offshore. He got to know some animals individually, such as 'the monster lobster that lived on the reef for many years. It's gone now, and I think it probably died of old age. It was the biggest lobster I've ever seen: its pincer alone was 11½ inches [29 centimetres] long. He lived in his own "monster's cave" and didn't tolerate another lobster on the reef.'

Another monster of the deep was a conger eel that lived in a particular crack in the rock, and grew bigger and bigger over the years. A friend of mine wanted to film it, so we tried to coax it out by feeding it with mackerel. But the first time, instead of coming to the fish I was holding out, it dived between my legs, over my shoulder and grabbed the bag with six more mackerel inside! Eventually it got so used to being hand-fed that it regarded anything you held as fair game. I nearly lost the lens of my camera that way. I'd just taken the close-up lens off the camera when up came this great mouth and tried to seize it. I had to give it a sharp tap on the snout to send it packing. We stopped feeding it after that!

Diving on the Cornish coast brings one close to the little-known world of shoal fish, and their sometimes staggering numbers. Ray recalls one occasion when: 'We were on the reef waiting for the tide race to stop running and saw a line of grey mullet, about 1 foot [30 centimetres] long, nose to tail. They passed us in tens, fifties, then hundreds, until there was this great "tube" of fish about 20 feet [6 metres] in diameter moving over our heads. They were still passing over when our air ran out, 40 minutes later. We swam right inside the shoal, with fish brushing against us. I tried to keep up with them, to get a feel of what it was like to be a grey mullet, but they were going so fast it was like swimming backwards. We made a rough estimate of the number of fish in that shoal and reckoned it to be over two million! It must have measured over 3½ miles [5.6 kilometres] from end to end and weighed around 9000 tons [9144 tonnes]. So Jonah's got nothing on me!'

While Ray Dennis watches life beneath the waves, naturalist Nick Tregenza looks down on the sea from a coastguard station on the cliffs. Sea-watching, as it is called, is the best way to detect porpoises (called 'piffers' in Cornwall from the characteristic sound, 'piff', which they make when surfacing to snatch another breath of air) and also the dolphins that are Nick's particular interest. Dolphin-spotting needs keen eyes and boundless patience.

You stare at the sea, and search and search, and try to hang on to the belief that dolphins are out there somewhere. You've been wearing your eyes out for ages, and then suddenly you see the shape you're looking for. It really hits you, makes your brain sparkle, and you just can't believe it at first. Then, with luck, the animal reappears, and you can follow it for a while, get a real sense of what it looks like and how it moves. It's very exciting – when it happens.

In the meantime, there are other things to watch: the fulmars 'wheeling like ski instructors'; the gannets, which the Cornish call 'zethers' or sea-arrows, plunging into the shoal they have detected from on high; or the odd rare sighting, such as a sunfish 'like an inflated plastic bag' floating on its side as it rides a warm current from the South Seas.

Rock pools revealed by low tide on the beach near
St Michael's Mount.

But it is the dolphin – either common or bottle-nosed – that most rewards the long hours that Nick Tregenza and his group spend staring out to sea. Nick's obsession with these beautiful sea-mammals began as a boy when he chanced to spy 'a school of dolphins riding high, conveying a tremendous sense of speed and power'. Sometimes he can get to know particular dolphins as individuals. One famous Cornish dolphin was given the name Beaky. As well as his friendliness, Beaky could be recognized by the bullet hole in his head where a Welsh fisherman had shot him, without apparently doing him much harm. David Chapple has fond memories of Beaky.

He lived off Mousehole by the lifeboat slipway, and every morning I went fishing, he would come up to give you a look and a snort. He'd then disappear, I assumed to feed, but he'd be back later, wanting to play. I wasted hours playing with that dolphin. I'd throw a beach ball, and he'd turn his head to go and fetch it. They say that his sonar was sensitive enough to see me, the engine and the ball. When you went to retrieve the ball from the boat, you had to decide whether you'd pick it up from the left or the right. He'd let you get right up to it, but just when you committed yourself, Beaky would pop up and flick the ball away. He seemed to be laughing at you. He'd take the ball on his nose and push it along at a great rate of knots. He also loved pulling lobster pots, and pushing the floats around. And he would always inspect the pots for their contents.

Unfortunately, dolphins and porpoises are constantly at risk from modern fishing nets and from the propellers of trawlers, and a great many were washed up dead in 1990 and 1991. It is possible too that dolphins have suffered from the accumulation of pesticides in their tissues from contaminated fish – as porpoises certainly have. But despite the hazards they face, dolphins are still a fairly common sight in Cornish inshore waters. Regular sea-watchers have a good chance of witnessing the never-to-be-forgotten spectacle of dolphins 'riding high'.

So far we have lingered in the sheltered, cosy world of the coves, on the beach and around the harbour, among the boats and fishing gear in the company of fishermen and sea-watching naturalists. There is another Cornwall beside the sea, the world of the cliffs and headlands, a much wilder place of natural rock-gardens and carpets of thrift, of gorse and bracken and rabbit warrens above the metronomic wash of the sea. Long sections of the Cornish coast now belong to the National Trust, many of them acquired under the Trust's Operation Neptune, launched in the 1960s to secure the best stretches of wild coast from unsightly development. Leslie Hicks, the National Trust's warden for the Polruan area, is proud that 'we've kept our bit of coast more or less as it is. As far as you can see, this is all National Trust land – a place of peace and quiet.' To keep the clifftop 'as it is' is hard work. 'You're expected to deal with anything that comes your way: fixing windows, planting trees, cutting the grass, repairing the paths and putting in stiles on all the walls.' Leslie has even invented a special walk-through stile for dogs! Much of this work used to be done by the now non-existent farm labourer in his spare time. 'That's what kept the bracken at bay, and why we had primroses and campions and violets. Now that there are fewer people on the farm, that has stopped, and wildlife has suffered as a result.'

The rise of undergrowth is one reason for the demise of at least one inhabitant of the wild cliff headland, the Cornish chough. A small, glossy black crow with bright red legs and bill, the chough became a symbol of Cornwall, although it was probably never very common here. According to the naturalist Dick Treleaven, even in their heyday there were not more than twelve pairs of choughs in the whole county, and many Cornishmen may never have seen one. The chough is a bird with charisma, known as a fire ram from the popular belief that it could carry fire in its bill. Dick's grandfather kept a tame one, inevitably called Darkie, in a cage. 'It was always pecking through the bars, or pacing up and down making a terrific noise.' The last Cornish chough disappeared in 1971 and was never seen again. It probably died of old age. It had lived as a lone widower, having lost its mate many years before to a peregrine falcon. However, the underlying reason for the chough's departure can be found in the overgrown state of its clifftop habitat. Formerly, the wild coastline between the fields and the cliff was kept short and grassy by hardy breeds of sheep which grazed there and enabled the chough to probe the ground for worms and grubs. Well-grazed headlands and coastal valleys also benefited another natural icon of the Cornish coast, the large blue butterfly, which also declined into extinction in the 1970s. The release and successful establishment of Swedish large blues on one or two carefully prepared sites gives some cause for hope in the case of the butterfly. But Dick Treleaven is not optimistic about any similar expectations for the Cornish chough. 'If you bung a reared bird out on to the cliffs to face peregrines and ravens, it won't stand a chance!' Cornwall needs a new avian symbol.

TOP The chough, also known as 'the Cornish daw',
now, alas, only a memory on the wild cliffs of Cornwall.
ABOVE The large blue butterfly and its food plant, wild thyme.
RIGHT 'The smack of breakers upon windy rocks':
a breezy day on the coast in late spring.

Perhaps it will find one in the peregrine falcon, which has made a spectacular recovery and returned to most of its traditional sea-cliff nesting sites. Peregrines were labelled a public enemy during the Second World War, in the belief that they represented a threat to messenger pigeons. Local author and naturalist Roy Phillips recalls that 'the first peregrine I ever saw in Cornwall was a bird captured by RAF falconers. They kept it in a cage, and were showing it to the people of St Ives as a bird to shoot on sight! We were told that killing peregrines would help to save our airmen. If the aircraft was shot down, the pilot was supposed to release a pigeon just before the plane crashed. Or so we were told. I suspect it was just propaganda and a morale booster, because no one in a burning airplane would have time to write a message and attach it to a pigeon! But during the war you'd believe anything, including eating more carrots to see in the dark.' Peregrines suffered another severe set-back in the 1950s and 1960s when they and their eggs became contaminated with DDT and other pesticides. In many places, they no longer breed successfully, and their numbers fell to alarming levels. For years it seemed that the peregrine was yet another lost species, and so it was tremendously exciting to see one pair, and then another and another, reclaim their ancient nesting grounds. Today there are probably as many peregrines as the Cornish cliffs can hold, and they are beginning to breed in quarries inland. They remind us that nature can flow as well as ebb. With a more tolerant attitude to birds of prey and the banning of the worst agricultural pesticides, this magnificent bird is once more a day-to-day spectacle in Cornwall.

Today there are sometimes disappointments in store for those who remember the golden Cornish sands, untouched by oil and without the imprint of a single foot, of flower-decked lanes unsullied by the dust of passing traffic. Nora Morgan is one such person.

After a long interval I returned to Cornwall with my husband, anxious to show him all the little coves and villages I remembered as a girl. Alas, how things have changed. The harbour where we used to go early in the morning to meet the boats coming in and buy fresh pilchards had become, of all things, a car park. Even the coves are spoiled by blaring transistors and screaming children rushing around with overloaded ice-cream cornets (which were in turn being picked off by squabbling gulls).

Dick Treleaven misses being able to take a picnic up on to the cliffs with the certainty of not seeing a soul there.

> In the evenings at Polzeath it was absolute solitude. There were far more undisturbed places then – and few bloody car parks, thank God! Everything seemed much wilder, with less erosion and not a tenth of the people you see today. Now the quiet of every cove is interrupted, and there's congestion everywhere. Everything is geared towards car-owners, whereas before you could take a bus to Bude or a train to Padstow. You can sum it all up in a word: commercialization.

One wonders too how the traditional virtues of the Cornish character – shrewdness, self-reliance, practicality and, above all, an inner sense of calm – will fare in the coming years. Lewis Butters has his doubts about the 'me generation'. 'To my way of thinking, people aren't as contented as they used to be. We had nothing. We couldn't have it, and you accepted it. There's a different kind of people today. They want this, and they want that, but we never had nothing.'

Some things, though, don't change. Leslie Hicks has the last word.

> I love this place and its peace. I couldn't live out of sight of the sea. I've been dragged – and that's the right word – off to London a few times. It was nice to see Nelson's Column and Westminster Abbey and things like that, but I could never be myself there. The young lady secretary said that they would pay my expenses if I wanted to catch the fast train up, but I told her I wasn't a bit worried about the fast train up, I wanted the fast train back! I feel sorry for people who live at that pace of life, going flat out all the time. I think if you've got a contented mind, there's no need to worry about what other people are doing or earning, so long as you're getting by. I'm glad I was born in 1930 and not 1990.
>
> The thing I like to do most – when the sea is boiling and the wind is howling over the cliffs – is to walk down to the beach on my own. I like talking to the tourists, but also I like to be alone sometimes, even if it's only for 10 minutes. Then I can say to myself, 'This is mine, this is my home, and I don't want anything else.'

POSTCARD

— Chapter Three —

How Black was my Valley

THE MINING VALLEYS OF SOUTH WALES

— Chapter Three —

How Black was my Valley

THE MINING VALLEYS OF SOUTH WALES

THE WELSH VALLEYS are green again. Sometimes a different shade of green – the deep, needle green of the conifer plantations or the suburban green of the housing estates and contoured land, rather than the oak woods and pastures remembered by the author of *How Green was My Valley*. The Welsh valleys were never entirely black. Dan Driscoll, who was evacuated from Cardiff to Aberdare during the Blitz, felt as though he'd arrived at a kind of earthly paradise of fields and trees and wildlife. 'A friend of mine, John Foley, said: "What do you think of this place then, Dan?" I told him I thought it was marvellous. "Do you know that God came from this valley, Dan?" I said, no, I didn't know that. "He did. There's a place down the road called Godreaman, and that's where he lived." I wasn't surprised. It was a beautiful place.'

Yet not far from the place where God had lived were the more familiar scenes of the mining industry: grim views of slag-heaps and winding gear, rows of terraced houses, and those eternal neighbours, the dust, the smoke and the smog. The tips dominated the landscape, files of dark pyramids along the sight-line,

The greener face of the Rhondda valley – a landscaped
slag-heap like a step pyramid above Stanley Town.

The colliery at Cwmparc in the Rhondda valley,
during the 1960s.

above the roofs of the terraces. With appropriate black humour, miners often referred to these man-made mountains as 'alps'. Their brooding presence seemed as eternal as the still, green hills beyond the horizon.

Every village in the valleys had at least one colliery. From first thing in the morning until late at night you would hear the bustle and banging from the pit: the winding of the head-gear bringing up the coal, and the cables passing overhead with the slurry. The whump-whump of the steam engines pulling the empties down and the whirr of the ventilator fan. The colliery hooters sounding the shifts (they all went off at once to let the New Year in). The steam trains passing up and down the valley, the coal-trucks going to and fro. The smoke pouring out of every chimney in every street. It has all gone now, or nearly.

The Welsh valleys were the place where the black wastelands of industry met the wild country – the hills, usually called 'mountains' in South Wales, the hanging woods and fast-flowing streams, and the windy, heather-covered moors. Little more than a generation ago you could find hill sheep wandering round the streets of mining villages and the farmer delivering the fresh milk on his horse and cart. When the miners weren't underground, they could walk in the hills (and they did – for miles) and race their pigeons down the valleys. It was true *rus in urbe* where the country rubbed shoulders with the town, the greenest of countrysides and the grimiest of townscapes.

Working in the mines represented most of the work to be found in the valleys. It seemed inevitable that the sons would follow their fathers down the pit after they left school. It might have been difficult to envisage any other future. So close were these communities that a decision to move elsewhere would not be taken lightly. Mining was a way of life, and had been so for generations. Hywel Morgan broke the family mould by becoming a schoolmaster, but his father was a miner all his life and his great-grandfather, David Davies, had entered the *Guinness Book of Records* as the longest-serving underground worker in history – an incredible seventy-three years.

His original name was David David. But there were two boys with that name in his class, so the teacher, to avoid confusion, called him David Davies. His record isn't likely to be beaten now. He started work at the age of seven, as a candle boy. He went down the pit carried on his father's shoulders, and his job was to hold the candle while his dad cut the coal. I remember my grandmother saying that the only time he saw daylight in the wintertime was on Sunday, because it was still dark when he went underground and it was dark again when he came up. There was no set retirement age then, and he worked till he was eighty years old. He died six years later.

Grafton Radcliffe started work in the pits in 1937, aged fourteen. Like most miners, he underwent no initial training or apprenticeship – 'Your training was your work experience' – and he was sent straight to the face as an assistant collier. His first job was loading coal on to the tram.

> We weren't allowed to use shovels. Because the screening equipment on the surface was very antiquated in those days, we were expected to clean the coal at the face. To do that, we used what was called a curling box, rather like a dust-pan and brush, only it was made of iron and was very, very heavy. We had to kneel and scoop the coal into the box with our bare hands, throwing out any bits of stone or other foreign matter. Then, once we had a box full of clean coal, we lifted it, carried it across to the tram, bent double, and tipped it in. Over and over again. It was hard going for a fourteen-year-old, with barely room to stand up straight, and so dusty you couldn't see much further than the man next to you. The face worker had his head-lamp, but all we had was an oil safety-lamp, which would detect gas but didn't shed much light.

Hywel Morgan's father worked in one of the drift mines. 'It was a long journey to the coal-face, more than a mile sometimes, bent double most of the way, and when you got there the seam could be as narrow as 18 inches [47 centimetres]. The only way you could cut the coal then was on your side, with a pick in your hand, and a shovel. You sort of cut it as best you could and threw it behind you. Sometimes there'd be water running past you. So by the end of the working day, you'd be thoroughly wet and cold, as well as tired.'

Grafton remembers the eerie sounds of the pit in the days before power tools drowned out other noises. You could sometimes hear the miners working in the shaft overhead, separated by a few yards of limestone and shale. 'When we were working the night shift, we could hear the earth waking up at dawn – that's how we knew it was daylight. Don't ask me to describe it. But we knew.' Another sound was that of water, not just splashing underfoot but dripping through the roof on to the miners' backs. Then there was the rattle of the trams on the rails, linked together in a train called the 'journey', ferrying the coal from the face to the lift. They represented another underground hazard:

> The trams travelled at 15 to 20 miles [24 to 32 kilometres] per hour and carried up to 3 tons [3 tonnes] of coal. So when you see that coming at you, you'd better get out the way. We had more killed and injured from trams jumping the

A Welsh coal-face during the inter-war years,
when the props were made of local timber and the face-workers
hacked at the coal with picks.

tracks than from any roof falling in – maybe one accident every five or six weeks. The tram was drawn along by winch, you see, by a man operating a distance away, who couldn't see what was happening. The only way you could stop and start it was by a phone signal from the tram rider.

Now, when the men were walking along the roadways to the coal-face, the trams were supposed to stop to let them walk in safety. But they rarely did. And in addition to the danger of trams derailing, there was the threat of the steel haulage ropes. As the tram clattered round the corner and up the slopes, the rope would lash from side to side, or from floor to roof. I remember one occasion when the journey came to a stop and there was a dead man inside one of the trams. He'd been caught by the rope and knocked into the tram. He'd been killed instantly of course – the rope had literally cut him in half.

According to Grafton Radcliffe, the pit ponies seemed to be valued more than men. 'If a man was killed underground, they'd lift his body aside and carry on filling coal. But if a horse died, all hell would break loose, because they would have to buy another one. Horses cost money, men cost nothing.' The replacement of the pit pony with the winch was one way in which technology increased the productivity of coal but not necessarily the welfare of the miner. Another was the introduction of the mechanical coal-cutter in the early 1930s. These machines operated rather like chain saws, cutting through the coal-seam as though it was plywood. And they greatly increased the level of coal-dust in the air, some of which was inevitably breathed in by the worker. Once the dust was in your lungs, it stayed there, as Ivor England recalls.

> The cutters had a fearful reputation, believe me. We called them the widow-maker. You just imagine this huge saw going in under the coal-seam and then literally pulling itself up the face. There was so much dust produced that all you could see of the man next to you was his lamp. Our faces got so black you had to wipe the muck off the inside of your lips before you could eat your sandwiches or drink your bottle of tea. Men came up after their shift blackened and curtained in dust. I come from a place called Ferndale where there was an epidemic of silicosis from before 1914 right up to the 1950s. There are still men dying of silicosis in these valleys as a result of the heartless attitude pit-owners had towards the introduction of machines like this. Even the horses got it.

Ivor England felt a burning sense of injustice, even as a child. Originally a coal-face worker, his father had been forced to become a surface worker on a lower income after contracting an eye infection. One day, working in the coal-yard, he was crushed between two drums and injured. But rather than take time off at half-wages, he was back at work the next day. With a family to support, he felt he had to. Ivor's father took part in the General Strike of 1926, when the miners were eventually driven back to work after six months by the threat of starvation, to conditions no less inhuman and, in some cases, even more badly paid. Those years were terrible ones for the miners, and the Great Depression made them even worse. Alan Pickens remembers his father coming home, his face all black – there were no pit-head baths then – washing his hands, and sitting down to dinner. 'You could see him falling asleep as he ate his dinner, having given his all, like. And the part that really sticks in me is that he worked so hard, and we certainly didn't live a high life, but we were still in debt. It didn't seem right to me at all.' 'It is ingrained in them,' believes Ivor England, 'this sense of bitterness. It was passed on to their sons, to virile young fellows like myself. We felt this great compassion for what they had suffered in those years. I felt, you know, that there must be something better than this for these people, that there was something seriously wrong with a society that let such things happen.'

The miner's one perk was concessionary coal, which was dumped by the coal-lorries on the doorstep at the rate of 1 ton [1 tonne] per month. Coal from somewhere deep beneath his house heated the boiler for the miner's tin bath, and kept the home fire burning in the grate all year round. But once he was laid off work, the supply stopped. Tydfil Thomas remembers the Depression, and the unemployed men combing the tips with sacks and boxes, looking for small coal. 'You'd see them going down the slope with the sacks over their shoulders. They were desperate men, because unless they managed to scavenge coal in this way there was no source of heat for warmth and for cooking. I also remember a little boy from across the road knocking on the door and asking my mother to keep the fat from the sausages she was frying so they could spread it on slices of bread to have something tasty to eat for lunch.'

When Alan Williams' mother had insufficient eggs to go round her seven children, she'd hard-boil them and cut them in half. 'So we had half an egg each for breakfast. When I told that story to my own children, it gave them a good laugh, but I don't think they believed it.'

Education offered a means of escape for some, and a means of doing something about pay and conditions for others. From the early years of the present century, miners' institutes were built in almost every village in the valleys. Fine, imposing buildings many of them were, subsidized by the miners themselves and sometimes built by coal company masons. The institutes became the focal point

OVERLEAF A scene during the Depression.
Unemployed men comb the coal-tip near Abertillery
for small pieces of coal.

of the community, often containing a cinema and concert hall, and a room for the billiard tables. At their heart, though, was the library, crammed not only with the usual diet of fiction but with reference books on every subject under the sun. Dan Driscoll remembers them well.

> The valley people had a different culture to the city people, to the people of Cardiff. They read books, and a lot of them were learned. You could see an old collier, who was face-and-frame vandalized by coal, and he could philosophize, he had read Cicero and Plato and understood Bertrand Russell. And he could speak in Latin, too, and these were ordinary boys that worked underground. It was their only way out, you see. One of the big exporting industries of the valleys was schoolteachers, to the Midlands, London, everywhere. There was a deep-seated ambition to learn, to go down to Cardiff University, and you saw it in the activities, in the cultural life of the valleys when I was a child.

One motive behind the libraries was the miners' desire to give their sons the chances that they had never had themselves. But there was also a thirst for education for its own sake, encouraged by chapel and the eisteddfods. Most miners had left school at fourteen or even earlier. Evening and weekend classes became popular, some run by the University of Wales. 'If you weren't there early,' remembers Alan, 'you couldn't get in. I used to attend one on classical music – a very popular one, mainly youngsters, and all of them miners.'

Music was, of course, an important part of this tradition, the product of Methodist hymns and inter-village rivalry and the innate Welsh love of singing. Most valleys had their own choral society and brass band, an essential aspect of any ceremonial from festivals to political marches. Ivor England learned to play the tenor trombone in his boyhood and joined the Lewis Merthyr colliery band. 'One reason I joined it was that the band players were all allowed to work on the surface, unloading timber and so on, so it wouldn't damage their lungs. But after a bit we got a new manager who wasn't having any of that, and all of us young-sters were sent underground.' It didn't stop him playing, though. Ivor was part of the band that won the national championship in 1974, and performed in the Albert Hall.

Today, nearly all the miners' institutes have closed. One was saved from demolition by the Museum of Welsh Life, moved and rebuilt brick by brick as a

The Lewis Merthyr Workmen's Institute Band,
photographed in 1950.

tourist attraction, a reminder of the cultural side of valley life. Some have been converted from educational establishments to clubs, losing their books in the process. Ivor remembers the fate of the books of the Lewis Merthyr institute, piled into skips outside. 'Economics, philosophy, politics … Those books had helped one boy become a qualified doctor, another to get a degree in mining engineering, and a third to become principal of a technical college.' What has happened to the old thirst for knowledge? Hywel Morgan thinks he has the answer.

I don't think they have the same incentive to work hard, these days. There was a time when I could tell my pupils that if you worked hard and passed your examinations and got your qualifications, you were sure of a good job. But you can't be sure of that any more. I know of university graduates who can't find

work. If somebody applies for a teaching post, they might say, 'Well, we'll take you on for a term, or maybe for two terms or a year.' And the reason for that, of course, is that they don't know what their budgets are going to be, whether they can afford to keep the teachers on. So the incentive isn't there now for people to go into the teaching profession.

Many miners were never happier than when rearing and racing pigeons. The acknowledged champion of this world is Billy 'Taffy' Bowen, who has held every office and won every major trophy going. To pigeon-fanciers he is a living legend. I asked him why racing pigeons is so popular in the valleys.

Well, the only industry here was the pits, and if a man goes down early in the morning, he's coming up again in the late afternoon. You've got to have something to do, and somewhere to go that doesn't cost much. And it's good to be out in the fresh air after being underground, you know. With pigeons, they can come up here to the loft, and sit and enjoy the sunshine. But the biggest thing is the bird itself. Once you get interested in pigeons and breed them, see them coming back of their own free will – it's a tremendous feeling. I suppose you could compare it with flower-growing, getting pleasure out of seeing the flower and the result of your work. Pigeon-fanciers are dedicated people, they love their birds. There are no losers in the pigeon game, you know. Everyone's a winner when his bird comes back. And there's always next time, isn't there?

The secret of success with pigeons, according to Billy Bowen, is simple. 'To race pigeons, you've got to think like a pigeon. You have to motivate your bird to win, and there are various ways of doing it. Through jealousies, or playing about with their nests, control-feeding them. But the main thing is the fitness of the pigeon himself, fitness on the day. Only that can win races.'

The valleys are not ideal for racing – since the birds follow the natural contours of the valley, these help them to navigate but at the same time divert them from the most direct route. Another problem, Billy would contend, is the pigeon's natural enemies, particularly the peregrine falcon. When the peregrine was about

The peregrine falcon, sleek assassin of the miners'
racing pigeons.

to be protected by law in the 1950s, Billy Bowen protested to the Home Secretary that it wasn't logical to protect both the birds and their predators. There are more peregrines in the valleys now than there were then, and some pigeon-fanciers claim that they tend to kill the boldest and most valuable birds, the ones that are out ahead of the pack. Even the most zealous of conservationists might feel some sympathy for the pigeon's owner when this happens, as Billy Bowen explains.

> When a man lets his birds out for exercise, these falcons come down and take them away in front of your eyes. You've seen the falcon take your bird and you run to it, and find it's still alive, you know, with its chest muscles ripped out. The falcon eating it before it's dead, that's bad enough. But when that pigeon belonged to you, when you've reared it, trained it, cared for it, and have high hopes for its sporting ability, you know; to see that happening in front of your face is terrible. It's like, we know that death in all its forms brings regret, but how much more regret does it bring when it belongs to you.

Billy Bowen isn't advocating a national campaign against peregrines, but wants the law changed so that fanciers can at least deal with the falcons on their doorstep, swooping down on their pigeons. Dan Driscoll, although a fellow fancier, is against this.

> Now, consider that the pigeon and the peregrine have been living together, cheek by jowl, for thousands of years. There are people who feel that the peregrine is a threat to the sport of pigeon-racing. Well, I've had pigeons since 1938, and of course some get taken; they're assassins in the sky, are peregrines. But far more pigeons are killed by guns or telegraph wires. I think the falcons have got as much right to that blue dome up there as the racing pigeons. They're one of God's creatures, and they're put here for a purpose, and I would be very sad if the peregrine was ever persecuted again, as it was.

Despite the poverty and dereliction of the valleys, many mining people have memories of a surprisingly happy childhood. Together with the closeness of a hard life shared came green hillsides and other open-air playgrounds nearby. Miners' children seem to have spent much of their free time out of doors, among the heather, the streams and the grown-over tips. Tydfil Thomas must speak for many Welsh children when she talks of the strong influence of the natural world on her upbringing.

I acquired any awareness of beauty that I may have from my early days playing in the woods and hillsides around the Cynon valley. I used to come to a particular place every spring to look for the early flowers, the violets, anemones, celandines. Later on we'd pick bunches of bluebells mixed with young beech leaves to take home to our mothers. I can still recapture the fragrance of those bluebells. As the summer wore on, the foxgloves came into bloom. I was quite an imaginative child, I suppose, because I really believed there were pixies living in the little caps at the top of the tall foxgloves. And at the same time, I also believed that emerging from the gossamer threads on a damp day like today would be little fairies, frolicking about. So this, to me, was a very special place, a secret place, I would say a magic place.

In the summer we'd climb down to this stream and build dams out of stone to make little pools. Once the pool was deep enough, we'd jump in with a splash, and of course the water was extremely cold mountain spring water, and we'd whoop and shriek with delight, splashing one another. Across from here, there was a stagnant pond where we'd come up with jam jars to collect tadpoles. We'd take them to school, and teacher let us keep them on the windowsill so we could watch them develop into tiny frogs. That's how we learned some of our biology. Nearby there was a spring where we'd make boats out of leaves – horse chestnut were the best – and drink the fresh, clear water.

My childhood days seem so carefree, compared with what children can do today. When I came up here with my friends, we were unaccompanied and had no reason to fear we'd be interfered with or molested. We played happily and freely, and our parents had no sense of anxiety about it. We loved the freedom it gave us, and I suppose, though we didn't realize it, it brought us back to the beauties of nature.

One popular game was to slide down the tips in a cardboard box, or on a tin tray. Daredevils could even whiz down sitting on the flat end of a shovel, with the shaft projecting out in front. Tydfil Thomas also remembers making little 'igloos' out of ferns in the corner of a stone wall. Once built, 'we used to crawl inside and tell gruesome ghost stories and frighten each other out of our wits.' The older boys

ABOVE Densely planted forests line the valley slopes in the
Rhondda, prompting mixed feelings in the local community:
'Little Switzerland' or a blot on the landscape? It depends
on your point of view.
RIGHT Foxgloves were among the earliest colonists
of the landscaped slag-heaps. FAR RIGHT The skylark, victim
of forestry and overgrazing.

played rougher games, setting fire to the grass to see who could make the biggest
blaze, messing about dangerously in empty coal-trams, looting birds' nests and
playing a painful game with a sharp stick they called 'catty and doggy'.

Then there was the picking of winberries (the English bilberry) in August,
when the hillsides were washed in a purple haze of berries. To Tydfil, these days
were the climax of summer, the warm pink of the heather, the bees collecting
nectar, and the miners' children out in their usual garb, woollen cardies for the
girls, caps and hobnailed boots for the lads, each with purple hands and a

'moustache' from the juice of the berries. Children would go round from door to door selling milk bottles full of winberries at sixpence each. For a few weeks, the whole village would be eating winberry tarts and winberry pies, with their exquisite, sharp-but-mellow taste which somehow captures the very essence of the moors.

Although it is natural to remember childhood as one long, carefree summer, many valley childhoods were in fact tightly regulated by religious observance. As a member of the Baptist church, Lena Charles had an unvarying weekly routine of chapel, prayer meetings, singing and recitation, though she looks back on it with fondness. There was an annual singing festival which was very thoroughly rehearsed, and an outing to Porthcawl. 'Though if the chapel couldn't afford it that year, we'd have a party in the vestry, with games and races.'

Is this mere nostalgia? Would we trade places today for these apparently care-free and innocent post-war childhoods? Vince Williams, for one, would not.

> Nostalgia's all right in its place, but it might be different if you were trans-ported back to those days, and suddenly found yourself with outside toilets that don't flush, and wash-days with boilers boiling away on open coal fires, scrubbing-boards and a big bath out in the yard where all the washing was done; iron mangles and bad-tempered parents, you know. No, you wouldn't really want to be back in those days.

The hillside arena for those childhood adventures has in any case changed out of recognition since the war. Many of the places where the children picked win-berries and built igloos and dams are now shrouded beneath coniferous forest in one of the largest plantations in England and Wales. There must be large parts, indeed, where no man has trodden for half a century. Most of the trees were planted in the 1940s and 1950s, and were intended to form the future source of pit-props for the collieries below. It was Lloyd George himself who is said to have struck on the idea of planting timber on the hillside to roll downhill to the mines in the fullness of time. In the event, none of these trees will be used in this way – the replacement of wooden props with hydraulic steel has seen to that. (Ivor England described that change as 'The best thing that ever happened under-ground – a steel roof above your head'.) Another reason for the conifers was to replace the thousands of acres of woodland cut down during the First World War.

Planting the trees was hard work, as Hywel Morgan remembers.

> It was all done by spade with a bag on your back containing 100 seedling trees. We worked up the hill, planting in furrows, following a row of stakes. Back-breaking it was, and on hard, stony ground, too. We planted Japanese larch or Norway spruce lower down, but above 800 feet [244 metres] and in the wettest places it was always Sitka spruce. We cloaked the valley in trees from top to bottom.

South Wales was considered a challenge to forestry, partly because of the prevalent risk of fire, partly because of the sometimes polluted soils. The stray coil of smoke rising on the horizon might have had any number of causes. It could have been the result of still-combusting coal waste, tipped from an overhead cable car, or farmers burning the hill to get rid of the dead growth, or boys setting light to the grass, or from a match dropped by a winberry picker who was smoking heavily to keep away the flies. Emyr Lloyd, who oversaw the planting of millions of trees in the Afan valley, remembers the potential violence of a forest fire.

> When you see one of these spruce trees going up, it doesn't just burn, you know, it explodes. There is so much turpentine in these trees, they go up like bombs, and it can be a very dangerous thing. I remember one cold Sunday morning in February, we had a turn-out to put out a fire. Some smouldering waste from an overhead cable had set light to the grass and, with the wind behind it, the blaze raced up the hill across frozen ground and into the plantation. It was burning at the rate of 10 acres [4 hectares] a minute, and we lost 440 acres [178 hectares] in less than three hours. Fortunately, in South Wales people turn out to help, you know, and the fire service and all the foresters around gave me their assistance. We beat back the fire with beaters made of old colliery belting.

In those days, the Forestry Commission tried to plant up every last acre of hill ground. There was one particularly difficult site, a patch of sterile hilltop poisoned by the fumes from a copper mine. Emyr remembers it as a 'moonscape', and that your feet sank into the dead, spongy surface. But, with skill and a lot of fertilizer, you can plant bananas in Piccadilly Circus. 'We used some alpine dwarf pines I'd found, and managed to capture the rainwater to irrigate the trees' roots. Each one was planted inside a square of turf folded back to hold the water and give it plenty of space. It was a difficult job but there are half a million healthy trees growing there now.'

Howell Morgan regards the forested valley now as one of the most beautiful in South Wales. It is known locally as Little Switzerland. His is not a universal view, though. Diana Phillips is saddened by the loss of what was there before the trees. 'It used to be such lovely moorland. You hear a lot of praise for the open moors in Yorkshire and Scotland, but not so much about Welsh heather, which was equally beautiful. Now what hasn't been destroyed by the conifers is being overgrazed by sheep.'

The local naturalist, Alan Pickens, also reminds us that although the forests have undoubtedly brought benefits for some wildlife, they come at the expense of what was there before. 'Everywhere you went on the hill you used to hear skylarks. And there were grouse in the heather, and hill birds like whinchat and wheatear. Then the forestry sprayed the area with something that affected the ants, and we started finding dead woodpeckers and didn't see so many small birds after that. There used to be ponds containing frogs, newts and dragonflies, but the forestry people drained them. I think the forest is mostly bad news for birds, though there are certainly more of the sort we don't want – magpies and crows.'

As the forest matures, and the first generation of trees is felled, it is beginning to mellow. It is more welcoming of people, too, now that the Forestry Authority is creating cycleways and glades as part of a more enlightened policy towards public recreation. The time to see life in the forest is early in the morning, or at dusk. A touch of light rain or even mist does no harm. With luck you might glimpse one of the goshawks which now nest, undisturbed, in the vastness of the forest. Vocal flocks of crossbills from Scandinavia may descend on you as they seek the cones on the older trees. Buzzards hunt rabbits and, less dramatically, earthworms, along the broader rides, and churring nightjars can be heard in recently replanted glades. People also come here to appreciate the changing sub-tleties of the forest in certain lights and certain seasons. Dave Connick speaks of the quiet beauty when the snow has covered the scars, or when clouds are rolling over the valley and you look down on a scene of swirling vapour, with tendrils of mist running along the streams like little fiords.

A less controversial role of forestry has been to help reclaim the slag-heaps and begin to sweeten the sour, polluted land. There was always plenty of both in the valleys, though the worst pollution of all came late, as the coal industry began to decline. This was caused by the industrial plant, built in the Cynon valley to manufacture the stove nuts known as phurnacite, by mixing and baking coal and pitch. Built just before the war, and extended in 1946, the phurnacite works effectively solved two problems in one go: it found an economic use for any bits of small coal that could not be sold, and it catered for the growing demand for smokeless fuel, especially after the Clean Air Acts of the 1950s. The phurnacite works recalled past industrial 'visions of hell', especially at night when the furnaces were opened and thick, sulphurous smoke belched from the chimney stacks. The people of nearby Mountain Ash called it Dante's Inferno. No one denied that the works was damaging the environment. People put up with it because the plant provided work for 2000 at a time of growing unemployment. But it was a dreadful neighbour. Vince Williams, who led the fight to close the works when the valley people had had enough, remembers the horror of it.

The men working the furnaces suffered from 'pitch warts', bits of hardened pitch stuck to the skin that wouldn't come off without a long soak. Eventually the company installed a sauna bath for them. There was a great fall-out of dust every night. If you wanted to do a painting job on your house, you had to wait until the wind was blowing in the right direction. Even the hill sheep were covered in grime. In wintertime we were plagued with what they called temperature inversions in which the fumes were held at ground level, and you'd wake up and smell the sulphur, and when you looked out of the window there was thick smog hanging over the whole valley. The dust killed the trees by blocking up the leaf stomata, so that the whole tree just suffocated. It seemed like the whole hillside had died. One day something poisonous got into the Abercwmboi lake, which was full of roach and perch, and suddenly there were dead and dying fish floating on the surface. It became known as the Black Pond. The local joke was that instead of the usual dawn chorus, you were woken up by a chorus of birds coughing.

What helped to close down the works in the end was the miners' strike of 1984–5. For a whole year, the collieries in South Wales came to a virtual standstill, and people got used to breathing clean air. So when the miners went back to work and the phurnacite works began to renew production, the campaign to close it acquired a new momentum of support, both in the valleys and in the towns. The people won, and the clean-up operation began at once. Relations have much improved, as Vince Williams explains.

> The company are now trying to show that they're good neighbours and can live with the community. They're enlisting the help of local schools to make the area attractive again. The children are bringing in muddy masses of bulrushes and various water weeds from another pond and establishing them along the lake-side. And the schools have come up with ideas of their own, like floating rafts where water-birds can nest in safety.

The phurnacite plant at Abercwmboi in 1969.
'A dreadful neighbour ... even the sheep were
covered in grime.'

The resilience of nature is evident again and again, as first one species and then another returns to the polluted landscape. Even the seemingly moribund oaks are producing new buds. Ducks have come back to nest on the Black Pond, there are enough fish to interest passing herons, and some people have even glimpsed a kingfisher. Diana Phillips, who lives nearby, has counted sixty-four species of birds in her garden – 'and that's pretty good for 1 acre [0.4 hectares] of land.'

The reclamation of coal-tips did not begin in earnest until a terrible disaster struck the valleys, one still fresh in people's memories, and which few people who were alive then can recall without tears. Aberfan was a name that entered the conscience of the entire country when, on 21 October 1966, a coal-tip slipped and engulfed the village school, smothering the children as they sat at their desks. Twenty-eight adults and 116 children died. There had been warnings but they had not been heeded. Coal-tips had collapsed before, and indeed the one at Aberfan had slipped to within 100 yards (91 metres) of the school twelve years earlier. This particular tip had been dumped on top of a natural spring. A week of heavy rain turned its interior into what Tydfil Thomas describes as 'a water bomb waiting to explode'. The avalanche of wet slurry fell on the school just after morning assembly, when the children had returned to their classrooms. Had they been in the hall, minutes earlier, they might have escaped. And, as Grafton Radcliffe reflects, 'If that damn tip had slid half an hour earlier, there wouldn't have been a child in the school.'

That weekend, long lines of valley people walked over the hills and stood in silence, high on the ridge overlooking Aberfan. The tragedy changed everyone's attitude to the tips, from the politicians and the Coal Board members to the lads who were experiencing their first taste of life underground. Suddenly the tips on the skyline were no longer tolerable. 'Up till then,' Vince Williams explains, 'tipping had gone on willy-nilly. Everywhere you went there was a tip on the mountain. If anyone objected, the Coal Board had tended to say, "Oh, well, if we can't have the tip, we'll have to close the colliery."'

People had got used to the huge piles of waste towering above their houses and gardens. After Aberfan, every tip was scrutinized carefully from the safety angle, and a programme of landscaping began. There was an absolute determination that such a disaster would never happen again. Millions of pounds were spent by local authorities and the coal industry on landscaping the valleys. Today, it is hard to find so much as a glint of coal through the greenery. The tips

ABOVE AND LEFT Aberfan. Views taken shortly after the
disaster in October 1966 show all too vividly how the tide
of wet coal slurry, like molten lava from a volcano,
slid down upon the village and engulfed the school.

were bulldozed to a minimum height, terraced and levelled. It is as if they have
melted back into the landscape. Some were resown, unimaginatively, with rye-
grass, others with more ingenuity, with natural contours and an eye to wildlife
and recreation opportunities. With the returning grass came field voles and
kestrels to prey on them, encouraged to stay by the artful construction of nest
boxes and perches. Today there are so many rabbits on the reclaimed land that

87

they are attracting the poachers. One of the last tips to be landscaped near Aberdare is now an attractive country park. There are plans to plant alders, oaks and rowans, to clean out the stream, to make it look as though the tip had never existed.

The Rhondda Heritage Park – one of the few reminders of the great mining tradition in this world-famous valley – uses the opposite approach. The Lewis Merthyr colliery was closed in 1983, but the head-gear still stands, and people can visit the mines in the company of ex-miners such as Gareth 'Busty' Mason and Ivor England. They are shown films about mining history and the Rhondda. They are reminded of rescues from flooded pits and fallen roofs; of the 1910 strike at Tonypandy when Winston Churchill sent in the troops; of the General Strike and the Hunger Marches; of the pride that all Welsh miners take in their heritage and in their memories. It was the miners themselves who petitioned the Coal Board to keep open this one pit to remind passers-by of the heroic days of coal, and to ensure they will not be forgotten.

Miners are, not surprisingly, bemused (to put it mildly) at the suddenness in which the Welsh coal industry has come to an end, in the public sector at least. As Gareth Mason remarks: 'Now that they've taken our work from us, the Rhondda's a lot cleaner. It's a beautiful valley, as lovely as anywhere in Europe. The trouble is, there's no work here.' But should people be reminded of what it used to be like? Is the passing of the coal age a matter for regret, or should we rejoice at the greening of the valleys? Vince Williams, for one, has few regrets.

Coal-mining has given a good living to people, but you've got to think of the cost. I have vivid memories of old miners on a steep street, clinging to a windowsill and fighting for breath to go a few yards more, and then hanging on to another sill. And though the outlook grew more enlightened later, you still had the coal-tips spread out across the hillside, and the subsidence which caused houses to crack and crumble, the blackened rivers, and the dirt and the grime. I'm proud of the valleys, and I'm very happy to see the industrial scars disappearing and the greenery evident everywhere you go. People come here now with the old ideas of the valleys as ugly places full of coal-tips and bare hillsides and dirty rivers, and they have quite a shock. I think that in time, and if investments come to replace the lost mining jobs, the valleys will be the better without it.

Ivor England, on the other hand, has this to say.

People ask how you can possibly talk nostalgically about coal-mining, about accidents, about men with silicosis. How can you talk about the awful conditions underground, walking a mile to a place that was soaking wet, or a place where the dust was so bad it was unbelievable. But the best way I can say it is this. When you went to work on a Monday morning, after a couple of pints the night before, you know – and I used to practise in the band on Sunday night, too – you'd go to bed late and get up at 6 o'clock. You'd go in the bus to the pit, clock in, go to the canteen and then to the pit-head baths; then you go into the lamp-room, decked out in your working gear, your lamp and helmet on, waiting to go down the pit. You might be going to a place that made you shiver when you thought about it, but there was the camaraderie, the friendliness, there was a great compassion of men working in conditions like that – the feeling that they'd look after you and you'd look after them. And the humour of the men – it was unbelievable. Going down in the cage, and on the walk to the face, there'd be jokes and banter all the way. I say if you weren't laughing there, there was something wrong with you.

IT SAYS SOMETHING about the islanders' perception of their home that the remotest inhabited part of the British Isles, the 'Ultima Thule' of the early map-makers, is called Shetland – not 'the Shetlands', and never, oh, never, 'the Shetland Isles'. The Shetlanders are not hermits eking out a living on rocky islets. They are a thriving community with a strong cultural identity, and they have inherited something of the roving spirit of their Norse ancestors. Shetland is a confident place with the inner strength to absorb even the revolutionary impact of North Sea oil. It is the 'south moothers' (as the occupants of the incoming boat from Aberdeen were called) who place Shetland in a little box on our maps and often, to add insult to injury, at a reduced scale so that it seems no bigger than the Isles of Scilly. Shetland is, in fact, both larger and further away than the map-makers lead us to believe. The archipelago of a hundred islands, big and small, that make up Shetland lies almost exactly half-way between Scotland and Norway. Until the thirteenth century, when Shetland was ceded to the Scots, it was Norwegian, having been settled centuries earlier by the Vikings. Even today, many Shetlanders regard themselves as more Norse than

A typical crofting settlement by a Shetland inlet.

91

Scottish – though neither, preferably: they have a distinct language and culture of their own.

Shetland is further away than you think – it shares its 60° of latitude with Bergen, Leningrad, Hudson Bay, the Alaskan coast and the southern tip of Greenland. Fortunately, it is warmed by the Gulf Stream, so much so that snow rarely lies for long and bitter frosts are unusual. But it is a place of the far north, of low light on the bare hills and the water, of long dark winters, short windy summers, of foaming breakers and shattered rocks, and green shores soon rising into the hill mist or, on clear days, to bleak, scarred moors where the only sounds are the wind, the wail of birds and the bleat of rugged, fine-woolled sheep.

Shetland is bigger than you think. There are 70 miles (113 kilometres) of mingled land and sea between Shetland's northernmost rock, Muckle Flugga, and its southern cape at Sumburgh Head. In terms of area, Shetland is roughly the size of Northamptonshire or Fife. But the human inhabitants are many fewer than those of Northampton or St Albans. About 17 500 fishermen, crofters and oil-rig workers live here, mainly on the largest island, which Shetlanders call Mainland, and on its smaller satellites, Yell, Unst, Bressay, Whalsay and Fetlar. The only town of any great size is Lerwick, with its sheltered natural harbour, solid grey houses and narrow streets. Most of Shetland is open, treeless space, a solitude in which to wander at will.

You cannot lose sight of the sea for long. Shetland scenery is an endlessly varied composition of sea, sky and land along a ragged coast that reputedly measures, if you count every islet and channel, 3000 miles (4828 kilometres). Here there are precipitous cliffs, thronged with seabirds; narrow chasms which scientists call geos; corridors of sea water known as voes; quiet lagoons and hidden harbours, sometimes with linking strands of white sand and pebbles. It is as if, Atlantis-like, the ocean had poured over and drowned an ancient landscape of vales and glens, leaving only the crests of the hills. Which is, in fact, exactly what happened. The voes and other strange ribs of sea that give Shetland its torn and tattered outline mark the courses of former valleys, worn into rocks long ago by rivers, streams and glaciers. No wonder that, until recently, nearly every Shetlander owned a boat. The sea is the natural highway here, and the boat was the Shetlander's car. Even the churches lie close to the shore so that the congregation could arrive in a flotilla of small boats, dressed in their Sunday best.

Shetland not only looks rather like Norway, there is an authentic Viking flavour to its place-names and language, too. You can hear the keen north wind and the billow of longboat sails in names like Scalloway, Housetter, Fetlar, Papa Stour and Uyeasound. Although the Shetlandic language is fast becoming a casualty of the cosmopolitan modern world, Shetlanders remind us each year of their birthright in their famous and splendid fire-festival of Up-Helly-Aa. It takes place on the last Tuesday of January, and is not done for the benefit of incoming tourists. Among all the fun and spectacle, the processions of torches, the burning dragon-headed galley with its oars and painted shields, the songs and dancing and Viking costumes, Up-Helly-Aa is a statement of Shetland's identity and ancient roots.

Rhoda Bulter, who sadly died soon after the completion of filming in 1994, explained what the Shetland language meant to her:

> Shetlandic, our language, is very important to me as a Shetlander. I feel that I cannot express myself *fully* in English or any other language. It's such a wonderful language. It describes things to you in 3-D and glorious technicolour instead of black and white. It adds another dimension to anything you say. I am speaking to you in English, but if I was able to speak in Shetlandic it would be far better. There are so many wonderful words, and it's so precise and exact. I think if the Shetland language is lost, then our identity is lost. It's what defines you.

But if Shetlandic is fading from the scene, something of its spirit survives in the dialect spoken by born-and-bred Shetlanders. What a 'south moother' notices immediately is the combination of stoicism and good humour. No one visits Shetland to sunbathe. 'Aye, it's blowing a gandy gooster now,' one Shetlander might say to another, as they go 'arling alang', that is, walking with some difficulty against the headwind. Rhoda Bulter told of the cheerful docker who met them off the boat from Aberdeen on a day that would keep most of us indoors.

> It was absolutely rainin' cats and dogs, it was really sheetin' rain – and one of the dockers tipped his hat as he went past and says, 'Now then, it's makin' a scar o' weet!' It means, literally, 'It's a bit wet,' and there was no complaint in it. The tendency nowadays is to say: 'Isn't this terrible weather ... Oh, look at the rain ... Oh, my goodness, when are we going to get some sunshine?' That just drags you down. But the docker, wi' a giggle in his voice ... now, he had the right idea. That was a Shetlander!

They joke too about the lack of trees (few trees, wild or planted, can stand up to Shetland's salt-laden gales). Rhoda's answer to complaints of barrenness was to implore the visitor to look more closely. In Shetlandic, tree and wood are much the same. 'There's the rumley tree – the bit of wood we use to clean the potatoes; there's the shapan which we use for mashing, and the gruel tree that stirs the porridge …' She loves the beauty and majesty of real trees down south, but thinks they would do nothing to improve the wide, clear horizons of Shetland.

Anyway, there are compensations. In the 'simmer dim', the night is replaced by a kind of drawn-out sunset, a glow like an ebbing bonfire in the northern sky. Ros Henderson describes those still, quiet summer evenings when the scent of the garden flowers wafts through the open windows, and the larks sing until midnight. 'The sky turns that magic red and yellow and turquoise. There are so many differ-ent colours in the sky all at once it takes the breath away. And it never turns to night, but stays that beautiful glow of orangey-red.' Even in winter, when there are only five or six hours of daylight and the evenings are long and dark, the big, open skies of Shetland can contain a kind of cold, calming beauty. Rhoda Bulter recalled the dark, dark country nights glittering with stars, 'which you feel you could reach up to and pull down'. And even on cloudy nights, the dark 'somehow seemed to envelop you like black velvet and caress you. You felt safe. You might see a light moving down and you'd think, "Oh, there goes so-and-so, I wonder where he is going tonight. I wonder if he is coming to our house."'

Andrew Williamson remembers actually looking forward to the winter as a child, and this was in the days before most crofts had electricity. 'We had paraffin lamps and peat fires galore. Like children everywhere, we were always delighted to get a bit of snow. The weather didn't worry us much. We dressed against it. There was always so much to do, like going down to the shore looking for wrecks, catch-ing rabbits, sailing little boats … There was a whole gang of us, all kids together. Everyone you met was a friend. The worst that could befall you was tumbling off a cliff, or overturning your boat.' Most Shetlanders seem to have fond memories of childhood.

Like islanders everywhere, Shetlanders have a strongly developed sense of community. As Gordon Walterson says: 'You manned the boats together, you

PREVIOUS PAGES Stormy seas lash the broken
cliffs of Eshaness.

Crofters knit Shetland woollens while
their menfolk fish the seas. Note the heavy stone weights
to anchor the thatch against the ever-present wind.

worked peat together. There was a lot of communal work on the land – setting
potatoes in the spring and autumn, cutting the hay. One family would help
another.' It is said that if the Orkney man is a farmer with a boat, the Shetlander is
a fisherman with a croft. It sums up the essential difference between Orkney, a
place of rich, fertile farmland, and Shetland where most of the land is sour, barren
and unyielding. There are few big farms on Shetland. The sheet-anchor of life was
the croft. And most of the crofts lie on the apron of relatively flat land around the
coastal bays and islets, with the limited good soil for cropping hay and planting

potatoes, turnips and oats, backing on to the rising hill from where tough little Shetland ponies brought in the peat on carts and in pannier baskets.

A typical crofter's house of the 1940s and 1950s had about four rooms: a parlour, a living-room and kitchen at the back, and a couple of bedrooms upstairs. The men were often away from home on the fishing boats, especially during the summer. Some, if they were in the Merchant Navy or on a whaler bound for the Antarctic, would be away for months at a time. The crofts, therefore, were worked mainly by women. A stranger might exclaim, 'How lazy! No men working.' But the simple reason was the men were all away at sea. One sees the crofting women at work in the black-and-white films of the period, weather-beaten, wrapped up against the cold wind in their woollen shawls, long thick skirts and aprons. Before the advent of the tractor, which few owned before 1945, crofters relied on horses and ponies or on their own two hands. There was a lot of digging – peat, potatoes twice a year, planting cabbages and turnips. There was many a weary march behind the plough. They had to make the best use of the dry weather in a never-ending battle against wind and rain. Few have rose-tinted memories of working the croft – it was toil. The romantic aspect was external, in the magnificent scenery, the sights and sounds of nature, and the sea in all its moods. But the crofters took pride in their patch. Teenie Garrick describes the croft in its summer heyday.

> Imagine the cabbage growing, and the turnips and the corn, growing up nice and green and tall. As you move along, you can see the potato beds in between, all covered in daisies, and the grass growing up along the edge of the corn. You would hear the drone of the bees and the little birds on the fence, and the skylark singing, and the lovely smell of the flowers. At the far side you would see the cows grazing.

Most crofts kept a few dairy cows for their milk and butter. To feed them in winter, they all made hay, and kept it in stacks close to the house, tied down with big stones. Haymaking in a cold, wet climate was quite an art. Ros Henderson remembers how, when the hay was about to turn yellow, the whole family would turn out with scythes and afterwards picnic among the delicious scent of the cut hay. 'To make the haystack, you laid the hay flat and put salt on it. The salt made the hay slightly damp, which seems to have caused the stack to generate its own heat, like a

Handploughing on a hill croft, preparing the ground
for a crop of oats. 'Only a Highland garron horse could work this
ground, ploughing only on the downhill journey then towing
it back up the hill.'

compost heap. My uncle used to thrust his arm into the stack every few days to
check that it wasn't getting too hot.'

Very few crofts today still cure and dry their own hay. The grass crop is now
mainly silage, cut by tractor-drawn machines. The haystacks have been replaced
by the less picturesque silage bails, covered with black plastic like giant dustbin
bags. While hay crops were taken from natural grassland, bright with clover,
buttercups, orchids and other flowers, the more frequent crops of silage come
from uniform green grass aided by large doses of fertilizer. The corncrake, whose
'crex-crex' call was once one of the sounds of the croft in midsummer, has been
unable to survive the change, and today no longer nests in Shetland. Indeed, crofting as a whole is no longer the mainstay of life; for most Shetlanders it has become
a sideline. And modern cross-breeds of sheep now munch the grass close to the
croft where once there were meadows full of wild flowers and, later on, flocks of
birds feasting among the stuble. In former times, the sheep were kept confined to
the hills. Today they are reducing what were once rich hay fields to pastures full of

rushes and rank grass. The crofts are still worked, but much of the seasonal colour has disappeared.

Not that sheep are a novelty in Shetland. There have always been sheep on the hill, and Shetland is famous for the fine quality of its wool and mutton. Shetland wool used to be as soft as silk – if you are very lucky, it can still be so – so fine in texture that you could knit a shawl and draw it through a wedding-ring. Joanne Christie attributes this wonderful wool to the hard life of the traditional Shetland sheep, a tough little animal that lambed on the hill and ate heather and seaweed. 'But if you raise the same sheep on short green grass, their wool gets heavier and coarser.' In the old days, the sheep knew their place, and it certainly wasn't on the croft. The quality of the wool might also have something to do with the old way of plucking rather than shearing it. This was called 'rooing', and it had the advantage of not damaging the threads – and also of leaving some wool on the sheep: a kindness at 60° north. Joanne explains how it was done.

> The new fleece grows underneath the old one and so, as it grows up, it pushes up the old fleece until it gets loose. So you get hold of your sheep, and tie its front and back feet together with a bit of rope. Then you lay it down, and the person who is going to do the rooing sits alongside the sheep. You don't pull out great handfuls – that would be painful. No, you have to be patient and pull out little bits at a time. It takes time – maybe half an hour per sheep – and some animals let go their wool easier than others.

The demand today though is for heavier fleeces and heavier carcasses and, with the rise in man-made fibres, for mutton more than wool. Many of the thousands of sheep on Shetland today are cross-breeds, and the emphasis is on quantity, not quality. They are less hardy than the pure-bred Shetland sheep, and the farmers have changed the landscape in their favour by reseeding much of the heather moor with grass. To Rhoda Bulter, the new-look hills seemed unnatural with their bright green patches and stripes next door to the brown and purple heather. Nor is the experiment invariably successful. 'A couple of years on and it's back to wild pasture again – but not to heather, unfortunately. That takes a while to grow back. Instead it goes back to rough burra and floss [the wild hard and soft rushes respectively] and nothing can eat that.' The wandering woolly hordes are also stripping the landscape of its colour – the wild flowers, and all that they mean in

'Rooing' the sheep by plucking out the loose wool by hand – the
secret of the incredible lightness of traditional Shetland woollens.

terms of defining the place and the season. As Mary Ellen Odie puts it: 'Sheep are
dirty eaters compared to the cow. Behind the cow it's all buttercups and daisies,
but the sheep leave rushes and nasty things, and eat all your nice orchids.'

On Shetland, wildlife is very much part of everyday life – you only have to look
around you. Crofters and fishermen do not, as most people tend to, see wild animals as something apart from their own lives – they would say that is an urban
concept. Crofters I spoke to talked about the songbirds and seals, the butterflies,
bees and flowers, as one of the greatest pleasures of a hard outdoor life. It is something we are losing, this rapport with our wild neighbours, this fullest use of our
senses. Ros Henderson remembers, for example, how you could forecast the
weather with your nose.

You can actually smell that summer's on its way, here in Bressay. If it's a
southerly wind, you will get the scent of the sea and the sand. In autumn, it's
different. There will be an easterly or north-easterly wind, and you get the smell
of moss. That to me is a frosty smell, a sign of winter coming. In midsummer

there is the heady, sweet smell of white clover. I used to lie down in it and listen to the bees buzzing. I'd fill a kishie [a basket woven from straw] with clover and put it in the cow stall for when they came home at night. It was their treat. Then there was the smell of hayfields and haystacks ... of horses ploughing the fields ...

A closeness to nature is demonstrated too by the continuing use of vivid local names for wild flowers. Lady's smocks, for example, which used to grow in great lilac bunches each spring, are 'water violets' or 'mudel dukkies'. Ros remembers the 'limmeriks' (bog asphodels) that grew 'like a golden fuzz' in the wettest parts of the meadow. 'I loved the dandelions, too – we called them the "sunshine flowers" – and the yellow "cra's fit" [crow's foot, better known as bird's foot trefoil] and the purple thyme everywhere.'

The birds, too, have their special names, with a Norse flavour. The 'caloo', for example, is the lovely, long-tailed duck that visits the Shetland coast in winter. The whimbrel is the 'pirri whaap' – that is, the small whaap, as opposed to the 'great whaap' or curlew. And 'dunter' – dunter-duck and dunter-drake – seems somehow just right for the homely-looking eider, the common sea-duck of Shetland. The less-loved black-backed gull is the 'beegie' or the 'schwabie': big and black. 'Bonxie' is in universal use for the bold, piratical great skua, of which more anon.

Many visitors come here to admire the magnificent sea-bird 'cities' on the cliffs and islands, and in the hope of seeing rare migrants, or Arctic species such as the whimbrel and red-throated diver that are more common here than anywhere else in Britain. And there is always the chance of seeing something rare and unpredictable, like the famous pair of snowy owls that nested on Fetlar for a few seasons. Watching the thousands of guillemots, razorbills, fulmars and other sea-birds clinging to the ledges of the mighty sandstone cliffs of Noss, it is easy to imagine that such exuberant scenes of life are eternal and changeless. In fact, the bird life of Shetland is in constant flux, responding to developments in the sea and on land, both natural and man-made. Both the gannet and the fulmar, which we might regard as quintessential northern sea-birds, colonized Shetland in the early years of our present century.

PREVIOUS PAGES Meadows of pignut and buttercup
overlook a shingle bar of tombolo along the beautiful coastline of Yell,
one of the northern isles of Shetland.

It may be the fulmar which prevents the peregrine falcon from establishing itself on the cliffs of Shetland because, as Bobby Tulloch, for much of his life the RSPB's representative on Shetland, explains. 'Fulmars have this revolting habit of emptying their oily stomach contents over anything that comes within spitting distance. They are particularly aggressive towards birds they consider to be competitors for space, and any bird of prey would come into that category. A mouthful of sticky fulmar spit means almost certain death for a bird like the peregrine which depends on its power and speed to catch its prey live. Once its feathers are stuck together – that's it.'

Bobby has seen the fortunes of many birds wax and wane in his time.

Bobby Tulloch

There was a big decline in eider ducks about ten years ago, from the high point in the 1970s. We don't know why, but it might point to a change in the sea currents. I regret the passing of things like the corn bunting. When I was a boy they nested in the rye-grass fields at the back of the house. I haven't seen one for ten years or more. On the other hand we've gained the reed bunting. They first arrived in Shetland in the 1950s, and nowadays they are almost everywhere.

A recent cause for concern has been the poor breeding performance of certain sea-birds, notably terns, guillemots and kittiwakes. Their staple diet is sand-eels, which they catch near the water's surface, and it is increasingly hard for them to find enough to feed their young. In the 1980s, Scandinavian factory ships trawled vast numbers of sand-eels to process into fish meal to feed to pigs and other farm animals. Bobby Tulloch is convinced that one need look no further to find the cause of the problem. 'It's like putting your sheep in the park, setting fire to the grass and then wondering why your sheep have died. The sand-eels are the grass of the sea – food for everything.'

ABOVE The Arctic tern, herald of summer, arrives in
Shetland on 21 May each year.
LEFT The sea-bird 'cities' of Noss, raucous and smelly,
the summer home of thousands of fish-feeding birds.

Others believe the problem is not so much the fishing as a slight rise in the temperature of the sea which has forced the eels to swim further down, out of the reach of terns and other birds. One thing is for sure. If the Arctic tern ceased to visit Shetland in the summer – and it travels 10 000 miles (16 000 kilometres) to do so! – many people would regret the passing of this little herald of summer. John Scott, who farms sheep on Shetland, told us: 'The Arctics always arrive on the dot, on 21 May. You can set your calendar by it. To us, it marks the start of summer, and if they didn't come I think it would take a chunk out of our lives.'

Of all the birds on Shetland, the bonxie is the hardest to ignore, at least at nesting time. It is a disconcertingly large bird, weighing about 2 pounds (0.9 kilograms), and feeds by mobbing and stealing food from gulls and other sea-birds.

Being dive-bombed by a bonxie as you walk over the moors in May or June is an experience not easily forgotten. But John Scott, whose sheep farm is in bonxie country, has learned to live with his avian neighbours.

> We had a dog that was driven into the sea by bonxies. But other dogs, like Peg, take a more aggressive attitude, and when they get dive-bombed, they jump up and chase them off. You have to take in the sheep at lambing time, so the lambs don't get attacked. But once the lambs are big enough, we don't have much of a problem.

Bobby Tulloch expands on this theme:

> I would rather be hit by a bonxie any day than an Arctic skua [a smaller relative that also nests on the Shetland moors and sheep-walks]. Some will squeal on the ground and try and lure you away from the nest. But they are so fast. A bonxie is a bit of a show-off. It will swoop within inches of your head and wheel off at the last second. But an Arctic skua will clip you on one side, and when you look round to see what it was, it will hit you on the other.

Fortunately, many visitors seem to enjoy the experience. There are not many places in the world where you get the chance to meet the bonxies on such close terms. Shetland's 5600 pairs represent more than half the total in the whole Northern Hemisphere, and it is therefore one of the species which the UK has a special responsibility to conserve.

You stand a better chance of seeing the elusive otter in Shetland than in almost any other part of Britain. Here, they roam in broad daylight along the shoreline and on the offshore islands – there are no broad rivers in Shetland, so the otters feed almost entirely on the sea. In the past they were hunted for their valuable pelts, worth a week's wages to a crofter. You can still find disused 'otter houses', that is to say otter traps, where otters unlucky enough to be caught were soon parted from their skin. Now that they are a protected species, otters have gradually become more tolerant of people, even to the extent of raiding garages and out-buildings. Bobby Tulloch puts out fish for 'his' otters, and sometimes when he goes to launch his boat an otter will jump out the other side. 'I sometimes find a nice big heap of otter muck in my boat in the morning – and it's nowhere near as pleasant-smelling as they say it is in the books. But I can forgive otters most things.' Incredibly, otters have even started using the stone jetties at Sullom voe, Europe's largest oil terminal. Nor is the otter the only animal that is 'tamer' than usual in Shetland. In Lerwick harbour there are seals that can be fed herrings by hand. There was outrage in Lerwick when a boy shot one of them.

Otters, seals, bonxies and Shetlanders have an occupation in common: they are all catchers of fish. Before the coming of North Sea oil, fish were Shetland's fortune. Boys were brought up on boat craft, on those special Shetland skiffs, clean-running, pointed at both ends, often built from Norwegian timber – the nearest supply. Andrew Williamson started sailing with his elder sister at the age of six or seven, and by his early teens he knew his way around the maze of land and sea, and where to find saithe, pollack and mackerel for the pot – with a wary eye on the ever-changing moods of the sea.

> We knew how to watch the tide, watch the wind, be aware of what was going on around you, be aware of what was dangerous – to get out of the place, and get out quick if you had to. The boys who go out fishing now will probably have a Norwegian fibreglass boat with a great big Yamaha outboard motor stuck in the stern of it – but they still go fishing. But we had to get out the oars and row for a couple of hours out and a couple more back, and get the sail up and sail. There's not the same intimacy with the sea now – with a small boat like that, you had to know the sea, and live by the sea and use it. Now you bash your way through it with your Yamaha motor. If you're young and stupid, it makes you more rash – chancing your arm. Familiarity can breed contempt. You're less exposed now, more protected, but you've lost that intimacy that you knew before.

The king of the North Sea fish was that 'silver darlin'', the herring, which was caught by drift-netting. Herring-fishing started late in Shetland, around 1870. Before that, the main fishery was cod, in the deep, cold waters towards Faeroe and Iceland. Herring-fishing was work for summer nights, after the ewes had lambed on the croft and before the harvest had ripened. The fishermen were at sea for up to six days a week, Monday to Saturday (but there was no fishing on Sunday). Mary Ellen Odie remembers the boats heading west out of the sound, perhaps twenty in line, with the wash streaming out in their wake. The hard part was finding where the herring were feeding. In the days before sonar equipment, and with

only a compass and the ship's wheel to steer by, the skipper used to look for natural signs. Fisherman Willie Henderson explains that you:

> ... looked for grease on the water, you looked for birds, gannets and mollies [fulmars] especially. They like the grease, you see, the oil from the herring that comes to the surface. That's always a good sign of herring or mackerel. Another thing you looked for was the colour of the water. Where the plankton was plentiful, the water was slightly red or green. And where there was plankton, there was likely to be herring feeding on it.

Another sign of herring was the presence of the minke whale, which the fishermen called 'the herring hog'. The herring hog was not in fact chasing the herring, but the herring's food, the ocean plankton. The 'hog' was regarded as lucky, partly perhaps because it sometimes seemed to drive the herring into the nets.

ABOVE Otters – 'tamer than usual in Shetland'.
LEFT A pair of 'bonxies' (great skua) warn a sheep and lamb
not to stray closer to their nest.

Another regular companion of the small inshore boats was the porpoise, as
Ros Henderson recounts.

> We used to see a lot of porpoises in the years after the war when we went out in
> the boat – we called them 'neesiks'. One night, there were so many neesiks that
> we got quite frightened – they were all around us, rubbing up against the boat …
> so many, we thought it would capsize. They were rolling around in the water –
> round and round just like black rubber tyres – the sea was alive with them. Since
> then, there's been a massive decline – we just don't see them any more.

Drift-netting for herring meant casting the nets just before dusk, preferably on a
quiet, cloudy night. Then, with a light at the masthead and the nets trailing out, the
boat would drift with the tide. At this point some of the crew might put their heads
down for a well-earned rest, before the skipper decided to haul in the nets at

111

around one o'clock in the morning. After a successful catch, and with the hold full of 'silver darlin's', it was full steam ahead for the market at Lerwick or Scalloway. But even in the great days after the war, by no means every night's fishing was successful. Sometimes you had the frustration of seeing the fish jumping on the surface but being unable to catch them. Apparently, if there was a moon and the water was clear, the herring could see the net – and they kept well clear of it.

Willie Henderson recalls one memorable occasion when they had been out for three nights without finding any herring.

> The skipper told me, 'You're steering – go where you want.' We took a course on the east side of Shetland, past Fetlar, and then after a while the skipper came up again and says, 'Where are you going?' And we says, 'We're going this way,' and he says, 'No, no, you're not, we're going to go that way.' Whether he'd had a dream whilst he was in bed, I don't know, but we turned and went down the west side. There was nobody else there, and we caught fifty cran [a cran is roughly 1/5 ton/tonne] of herring. They came over the side like a silver river – and we got a good price for them, too!

Packing the 'silver darlin's' into barrels at Lerwick
during the heyday of the fishing industry.

Alas, it did not last. In the early 1960s, suddenly and unexpectedly, the stock of herring plummeted. It fell so alarmingly low that the government was forced to ban herring-netting for six years. It was the end of an era. The big Norwegian trawlers – twice the size of the Shetland boats – had started fishing in Shetland water just outside the territorial limits, using big purse nets that could take more herring in a single haul than the Shetland boats could catch in a whole season. What is more, they could also catch herring in deep water by day as well as on the surface by night. 'They had these huge nets that were lifted by hydraulics,' says Mary Ellen Odie. 'They certainly gave us a lesson in how to catch herring. At the end of that season, the Norwegians had caught nearly 200 000 tons [203 200 tonnes], much of which ended up as animal feed. The British had caught about 10 000 tons [10 160 tonnes].' Soon, the great days of drift-netting were over and, with them, those long, lively summer days when the harbour at Lerwick was bursting with fishing boats, with the coopers hammering the barrels, the fishergirls in their overalls trimming the catch, the busy curing stations and processing factories, the street vendors and the banter of young people together, all now a memory. The harbour can still be lively – they say you can hear every language in Europe on the streets of Lerwick when the boats are in. But it isn't quite the same.

The picturesque steam boats may be gone, but Shetland retains a large, modern fishing fleet, and the harbour is still ringed with processing stations where much of the catch is quick-frozen. The boats are bigger now, with more powerful motors and sophisticated navigation and sonar equipment. Modern fishermen rely on electronics to navigate and detect their quarry, not herring hogs or grease on the water. They can detect fish without lifting their eyes from the controls. And they catch a greater variety of fish using deeper hydraulic nets – not herring alone, but saithe, mackerel, whiting, cod and plaice. Some fishermen, like George Walterson, are philosophical about change.

> We've had good and bad times, the same as any kind of job. It has its rewards, and in some years it's poor. A few years ago the weather was bad and we had a poor season. But you keep going, and it comes back. Sometimes the fish are very difficult to catch – but they'll come back if you put enough time into it.

In the meantime, there is oil. Newcomers to Shetland may be surprised at how little oil-related developments have intruded on Shetland's landscape. The land installations are tucked away in sheltered islets and bays and the drilling rigs are far out to sea, most of them beyond the horizon. The terminal at Sullom voe lies at one end of a long, sheltered arm of the sea, and the only good view of the largest oil terminal in Western Europe is from a helicopter. Oil was bound to bring a profound change to island life. Shetland was fortunate in having a council that foresaw the social problems that oil development would bring, and took steps to protect the interests of the islanders (and of visitors, too). Even so, the impact of oil has been immense. The old, self-reliant Shetland where, as Rhoda Bulter put it, 'if you were out shopping and met a stranger, it was news,' has gone, perhaps forever. Oil has brought in people from all over the world, and new types of people – businessmen, technicians and rig-workers with an urban lifestyle and money to spend. Shetland has suddenly become cosmopolitan, more materialistic – not more outgoing, because it has been that since the days of the whalers – but perhaps more like the rest of Britain, for better or for worse.

And, of course, it has become rich. Oil money is everywhere, and the standard of living is high. This sudden access of wealth has been managed wisely, on the whole. Shetland schools were always good, but now they are among the best equipped in the country. There is a big, new leisure centre in Lerwick, more and better sheltered housing and care units, grants to help the fisherman to buy a new boat. Money has created new jobs in the service industry, an elaborate tourist infrastructure and created excellent prospects for the young. Fortunately, despite the temptations of wealth, there is still remarkably little crime in Shetland. The younger generation – those who cannot remember a Shetland without oil – now take all this for granted. As Rhoda Bulter remarked:

> We didn't use to regard helping neighbours as a chore, it was almost a recreation. You'd hear someone say, '...we'll all go and help. Oh, yes, we'll look forward to that – we'll have such a spree!' Now, that attitude seems to be lost completely. And people wear longer faces – they complain about the weather, and complain about this and that.

The great fear of many environmentalists was that siting a large oil development in the midst of an outstanding area for sea-birds invited a major wildlife disaster. Such fears seemed fully justified when, on 30 December 1978, the *Esso Bernicia*, one of the first big tankers to come in, collided with the jetty at Sullom voe and

An aerial view of Sullom voe, the North Sea oil terminal –
'we barely notice it now'.

ruptured its fuel tank. More than 1000 tons (1016 tonnes) of heavy fuel oil poured out into the enclosed waters, painting the rocks and shores with sticky tar and killing practically every bird in the voe – black guillemots, eiders, shags, grebes, divers and long-tailed ducks. The white sheep feeding on the seaweed soon turned an oil-stained brown but, unlike the birds and some unlucky otters caught by drifting oil, most of them survived. Bobby Tulloch remembers finding sheep 'absolutely plastered with oil, and we were wondering what to do with them. But a few days later – amazing, every trace of oil had gone. Maybe it was the lanolin in the wool, so that the oil, instead of sticking, just fell off.'

The one blessing was that this oil spill had tested the contingency plans for sealing off the voe – and found them wanting. The pumps that were supposed to inflate the booms broke down, and so it proved impossible to isolate the slick. Millions of pounds were spent by the oil industry on better safety equipment. So far, the improved protection seems to have worked, but the threat will always remain. The oil company made a better job of cleaning up the mess than containing it, and today the waters of Sullom voe are as clean as ever. 'You wouldn't find so much as a plastic bag in there, it's splendid.'

Of more recent memory is the grounding of the oil tanker *Braer* during a gale in January 1993. This disaster had nothing to do with Sullom voe – the *Braer* was just a passing ship that was blown on to the rocks. This time, virtually the whole cargo – 85 000 tons (86 360 tonnes) of light oil – spilled into the sea as continued rough weather frustrated salvage attempts. A major disaster was predicted, but the same breakers that had driven the tanker on to the rocks also prevented a surface slick from forming. Some of the oil was blown clear out of the water by the wind, up over the cliffs and on to the pastureland above. It temporarily ruined the grazing, and the risk of contamination ended the salmon and shellfish industry on that part of the coast for the time being. Fortunately, the *Braer* story had a happy ending so far as the salmon-farmers are concerned. Much of the contaminated stock was bought by Norwegian mink-farmers – someone remarked that 'the mink had a good shine on their coats after that lot!' Insurance companies covered the remaining loss. All in all, the *Braer* disaster could have been a lot worse.

Shetland has absorbed great changes in the past half-century, more than at any other period since the coming of the Norsemen, and yet it has remained true to itself. The islands have not been vulgarized by oil and wealth, nor have the islanders altogether abandoned the old way of life. Ironically, some crofters are now incomers, repelled by the ugliness and the materialistic ways of the urbanized south. They experience the same arching skies, the larks singing at midnight, the scent and hum of the clover fields and the lofty stretches of bird-haunted moorland as those people who farmed these acres before them. It is hard to imagine that the spirit of Shetland will ever die, that rugged, hard-wearing optimism that has triumphed over Atlantic gales, 60° of latitude and all the trials and uncertainties of remote living. None of the people we interviewed would dream of living anywhere else. 'Everything that's needed is here,' said Ros Henderson. 'It's progressive and forward-looking, but still beautiful. It's my home. All you need to do is to walk out on a bonny calm night in the summer, when the sun is setting, and listen to the curlew and the larks … There's just that inner feeling, a magic all of its own … It's lovely, and it takes the breath away!'

Rhoda Bulter wrote a poem which sums up her feelings perfectly.

I seek not the place where the palm tree grows,
Or the brilliant insect hums.
Mine is the land where the north wind blows,
The land where the twilight comes,
Where the sky is bright with the northern light
When the shortening day is done,
And the icy wind speeds the migrants' flight
To the southland and the sun.
I long not for the spicy breeze
Of the jungle dark and green,
But give me the land where the waters freeze,
And the hills are brown and lean,
Where beneath the stars on a frosty night,
The pony looks shaggy and warm,
And the hare is wearing his winter white
In time for the first snow storm.
For there, when the spring returns once more,
And the streams are free to run,
I can wander barefoot along the shore
In the rays of the midnight sun,
And hear the beat of the raven's wings,
Like distant muffled drums.
Yes, mine is the land where the crowberry springs,
The land where the twilight comes.

POSTCARD

— Chapter Five —

Stonescapes

THE YORKSHIRE DALES

THE SYMBOL of the Yorkshire Dales National Park is a sheep. A black-faced, curly-horned, prize-winning ram named Rastus. He was chosen to represent the newly autonomous National Park in 1974, replacing the White Rose of York that the Dales used to share with the North York Moors. To some, a sheep might seem a strange choice for a landscape celebrated for its natural beauty, the rocks and pavements of limestone, the wild flowers and the birds. To others the sheep might be seen less as the glory of the Dales and more what is currently their main problem – too many animals, cropping the hills to the bone. The choice of Rastus was plainly a public relations exercise 'to compliment the farmers and bring them a bit closer to us', as Wilf Proctor, one of the first wardens of the Yorkshire National Park, put it. But it is for all that an appropriate enough symbol. The scenery we admire so much in the Dales was created by shepherds. By Cistercian monks, tending their vast flocks – the visible wealth of the glorious abbeys of Fountains, Rievaulx and Bolton; and by the farmers who built the spider's web of white stone walls to enclose the hay that fed the animals in winter.

The stonescape of Upper Swaledale: irregular walls,
solid farmhouses, outbarns and distant crags.

The Dales are a landscape where the present seems intermingled with the past. The language is broadest Yorkshire, but the place-names are ancient Norse. 'Dale' itself is a Viking word, as are 'fell', 'foss', 'tarn' and 'beck'. But the Dales are more than names on a map; more than a series of valleys in North Yorkshire. They are part of every Yorkshireman's soul, and the hoped-for earthly paradise of beauty and fresh air that brings walkers, cyclists and family cars by the thousand from Leeds, Bradford and Manchester. For Roger Nelson, a Wharfedale man: 'The Dales are in my blood. I always joke that we've got peat-water in our blood, but it expresses our heart – the millstone grit, the heather and the peat, the dry-stone walls and the rolling countryside. Whenever I'm abroad, my heart is still in the Dales. They pull you back wherever you are, and when you come home you feel yourself slotting back into position.'

Still, for all that, these are real valleys and real hills. How do you describe the Yorkshire Dales? A land of moods? 'It can be everything from the black sombre moods of winter and the sudden summer storms, to the more gentle moods when you can lie on a bank under the coomb and hear the larks singing,' says Mike Harding, the folk singer and comedian. Bill Mitchell, former editor of *The Dalesman* magazine, describes it as a place of horizons. 'It's not what the Americans call the Lake District – Gee Whiz country. The drama is in the skies and in the tones and textures of the land, and in the contrasts. There's Ribblesdale which is part bare rock, part lovely hills and pleasant woods, and little green lanes. There's Wharfedale, a long, romantic, brooding valley, with a wealth of folktales. And Swaledale, many people's favourite, small, homely, the classic Dales farming scenery. There's no wilderness at all in the Dales. It's a stonescape of dry-stone walls, of the farmsteads and the little outbarns, and villages that look half as old as time.'

Sir Anthony Milbank emphasizes the dramatic lighting of the Dales, the ever-shifting shadowland of light and shade, best appreciated from a lofty perch looking down into the valley. Roger Nelson talks of the physical evolution of the landscape, the glaciers that carved out the flat-bottomed, steep-sided valleys, the mosaic of millstone and limestone, flowery banks and peaty hollows, the hanging woods and uplands of heather and bracken. These are all valid portraits of the Dales. What

A scene in Upper Swaledale, typical of the rugged Yorkshire Dales with its wall-scape, an outbarn with its hay rick, little hollows and steep hanging woods.

we see in this landscape is in a sense the sum of our own individual responses to it.

As Bill Mitchell reminds us, the Dales are a farming landscape, despite their apparent wildness. To understand the Dales you must understand the Dalesmen (you would not get very far by calling them Dalespersons). What are they like? Is the image from the James Herriot stories – blunt, taciturn and tight with money – an accurate one? Up to a point, perhaps. Half a century ago, when tractors or even cars were in short supply, the caricature Yorkshire farmer 'who said nowt an' for a long while', the stage Yorkshireman 'wi' deep pockets an' short arms', might have been truer to life than he would be today. Working on the fell in all seasons and all weathers bred tough, self-reliant men, used to hardship and isolation. 'They were beholden to no one. If times were bad, they just used to curl up in a sort of semi-hibernation, and wait until things improved. They didn't want anybody else's help or pity.' It takes an effort now to recall just how isolated were the lives of those living in the Upper Dales (one thinks of *Wuthering Heights*). Roger Nelson remembers that his grandmother had once gone from Christmas to Easter without setting eyes on another woman. By the same token, those outsiders that entered these remote regions did so with a certain sense of adventure. They found people with strong characteristics, people who were 'close' and who spoke in strong dialects. The men, especially, could seem slow and suspicious at first. But once they got to know you, they opened up. Dales hospitality is famous – it originated in times when strangers were rare and were welcome as a source of gossip from the outside world. As Roger Nelson says:

> Once you've got a foot under the table, you're made to feel at home. Mind, some folk are never accepted, not in twenty years, while others, once they've been summered and wintered, as we say, once they've been tried and tested, they're accepted as part of the Dales.

Mike Harding is fortunate enough to be in the latter category. Brought up in Manchester, he moved to the Dales in the early 1970s, and inevitably became the object of local curiosity. His neighbours were all farmers, builders and quarrymen, and they couldn't work out how he earned his living. ' "I'm a folk singer and a comedian." "Well, tha' doesn't seem very funny to me." ' Then one day he took part in a fund-raising concert in Settle which a lot of people from the village attended. 'I did about twenty minutes of singing and story-telling. On the way back in the bus, they said, "So *that's* what you do." Uh-oh, I'm in for it now, I thought. "Yes, I'm afraid it is." "*It'll do.*" I thought, that's wonderful, a great compliment from a Yorkshireman. It'll do, you'll mend.'

Then there is the Dalesman's legendary meanness with money. That needs qualifying, too. Money was in short supply, and counting the pennies was no more than good husbandry. But in many cases, it was not so much meanness that was on display as a love of bargaining, as Sir Anthony Milbank explains.

> A Dales farmer will very rarely accept the first offer he's made. If someone is trying to sell him something, he'll be very reluctant to pay the first price, whatever it is. He'll try and beat you down, and I see nothing wrong in that at all. So maybe that has led to their reputation as being slightly mean. I don't think they are. They're very, very generous at the right times, but they don't believe in paying any more than they have to for anything.

A lot of the stories of the Dales revolve around the blunt sayings of local characters. Mike Harding has a rich supply of yarns about a Dales gamekeeper called George, a big, tall man with size 14 feet. There was the time, for example, when the estate most unsuitably gave George a Mini van to get around in. He went round to the garage to pick it up. '"Has tha got it?" "Yes, George, it's over there." He wanders over to the diminutive vehicle and stares at it for a while. "Where's the one for t'other foot then?"' Or the time when the doctor delivered his wife of twins. He shouts down the stairs, '"There's two lasses, George, one of them's white and the other one's black." "Well," comments George straightaway, "that's typical of the missus, she burns everything she puts in the oven."' Of course, such stories have to be told in the Yorkshire accent, familiar the world over. What is not often realized is that Yorkshire, and the Dales dialect in particular, is an ancient language, preserved from the dilutions and distortions of time by isolated living. The spoken English of Shakespeare's time might have been closer to Yorkshire than to Oxford, as Bill Mitchell explains.

> I've interviewed quite a few people by tape-recorder over the years. And sometimes, when I'm playing them back and making copies for articles, I'm aware of a special little intonation in their speech. Then I realized what it is: it's

the language of the King James Bible. They'd absorbed it as, Sunday after Sunday, they went to chapel and listened to passages of the Bible being read. Many of these people hadn't had much schooling, and so most of their education had been picked up by going to services and listening to sermons and to the word being read. The classic example is 'thee' and 'thou'. I heard one Dalesman say to his friend, 'Don't thee thou me,' before going stomping off. Obviously he was bringing to an end a conversation that didn't appeal to him at all.

We should note at this point that one dale is not the same as another. Very much not. There is a friendly – well, mostly friendly – rivalry between Swaledale, Wharfedale, Wensleydale and the smaller dales. There is inter-dale competition as to who produces the best cows or the best lambs. As Roger Nelson recounts: 'They say, "so-and-so from such dale always has good sheep," and he's respected for it. It's not easy to produce top-quality lamb year after year. You've got to be good at your job. And a lot of Dales farmers have got it, this ability.' On the social scale, Swaledalers tend to regard themselves as the toughest, with the broadest accents and the warmest interiors. Folk from Swaledale are apt to regard those from Wharfedale as a bit soft, not proper Dalesmen. At the same time, some Wharfedalers don't see Wensleydale as a proper dale at all, it being too flat and too 'civilized'. It is, of course, sacrilege to compare *any* of the dales of Lancashire with those of Yorkshire. Yet the rivalry is good-natured, and what matters most is the fact that you are a Dalesman. As Roger Nelson, a Wharfedaler himself with a Wharfedale man's bias, tells it:

> When you're describing yourself to outsiders, the first thing you want to know is whether they know where England is. If they understand that much, you say you're a Yorkshireman. All right so far? Well, then you tell them you're a Dalesman. And if they understand that, you say you're from Wharfedale. And if they know where that is, you can tell them that you're from *Upper* Wharfedale. You can't go any higher than that. You've reached the peak of human achievement.

The old distinctions and characteristics are becoming blurred as time goes by. With the help of the car, people mix a great deal more, and the old, close communities are breaking down under the onslaught of tourists and more permanent

A typical Yorkshire farmhouse in Cotterdale, built of stone
and slate with small windows facing the valley.

incomers. Life is in some ways freer and easier than it was. Fifty years ago, the
Dales villages were self-sustaining communities. Everyone knew each other, and
all the basic needs of farm and farmhouse were there. Indeed, the village was
essentially the service centre of the farm, as well as the social hub of that part of
the dale. Each had its own blacksmith, joiner and cobbler. There was often a
clogmaker too, a block carver of alderwood. You could readily purchase a pair of
clogs as recently as the 1960s, ideal footwear for working in wet fields, and one
recommended by doctors in cases of bad feet. Green welly boots killed the
Yorkshire clog trade. Kathleen Carlisle, a farmer's wife, remembers those wonderful village shops that sold everything 'from a reel of cotton to a loaf of bread and
your weekly vegetables. When my babies were little, the shopkeeper even weighed
them on her scales on a clean piece of paper, to save us the bother of going to the

125

clinic.' Milk came not in bottles but fresh from the farmhouse. People used to leave a can or jug at the farm 'cooling house' to collect later on.

Social life, too, was village-orientated. First and foremost there was the daily round of natter and gossip. As farm wife Edith Carr says, 'I think to be a Daleswoman you've got to be a friendly kind of person, the sort who will chat to anybody. I speak to just about everybody I meet and, it's surprising, just about everybody speaks to me.' Probably every village had characters like old Mrs Binks who, Ron Metcalfe remembers, 'used to wander from place to place pushing a pram with a big black cat on top of it. She'd disappear into a barn in the evening, and next morning, when you went to milk the cow, you'd find that a quarter of its udder had already been milked. The cat was beautifully black and shiny, and we all knew why. Mrs Binks used to sell clothes pegs, and small things like that; she ended up in the alms house at Linton. She was quite a fright to look at, and when we were young she used to scare us half to death.'

At the weekend there were young farmer's dances. 'If someone owned a van or a car,' recalls Kathleen Carlisle, 'we used to pile in, squashed together like sardines. If we couldn't get a lift home, we'd all walk back, arm in arm across the middle of the road. There was so little traffic then that it was quite safe to wander down the streets and lanes without any fear of being knocked down or run over.'

The farmhouse had a weekly routine; a set job for every day except Sunday. You could tell it was Friday when the delicious smell of baking came drifting into the street from each open window. Nearly every housewife baked her own bread and cakes, and pies, pastries and oat cakes were staples of life. You made butter and cheese mid-week, and there was often a particular day set aside for cleaning and mending. Then there was wash-day Monday, a day of toil and lather for Edith Carr. 'You'd boil the water in the copper, a couple of tubs' worth, and then there'd be scrubbing and rinsing and the old wringing machine, mangling and struggling away. Then we had a good year with the sheep, and lo and behold if I didn't get a washing machine. My husband got it second-hand from a chap who dealt in all kinds of stuff. It was an early Hoover, like a big tub with paddles inside. Well, clonk clonk, it was going round; gosh, it was an antiquated thing – but better than scrubbing away with a brush and rubbing me knuckles off.'

Like many villagers, Edith kept a few pigs to send to market or to salt down for her own larder. Obtaining a good price for a pig required canniness and preparation. Edith's own recipe for success was to feed the animal with balls of oatmeal mixed with milk. 'After you'd forced its mouth open with a stick and pushed one or two down its throat, the pig realized that the oat balls were a good thing, and it would sit there with its mouth open, waiting for the treat. You can tell a pig that's had the oatmeal treatment. Its hide has a lovely finish; and the bacon's sweeter, too.'

It was normal in those days for a farm to slaughter and butcher their own pigs. Carnivores of the 1990s have long become used to sanitized meat-counters, and prefer not to dwell on what might go on inside EU-approved abattoirs. Dales farmhouses could not afford to be squeamish, as Edith Carr recalls.

We used to lead them in from the pigsty in the yard into the back kitchen. Oh, it was a horrible job. We had a boiler of water going in the corner, and the sharpened knives laid out and this strong, flat table called a pig-stock. Well, the poor things knew what was coming, you know, and they were squealing away. Two or three farming neighbours would come in to help us to hold the pig down

Scraping the bristles from a freshly slaughtered pig
using boiling water.

on the stock. Then the knives would be flashing about, and all this gory work. The poor old pigs, we can laugh about it now, but it was a terrible job. We made a black pudding out of the blood, and my job was to put a handful of salt into the bottom of the tin, and keep stirring the blood to stop it from clotting. Meanwhile the carcass would have to be scraped – this is where the boiling water came in – and when you got the bristles off one side, you'd roll it over and do the other. Then the pig was heaved up on to a beam, and its stomach slit open to let the insides out, and it would be left to hang for a couple of days until it had gone really stiff. Then down it came, and on to the stock again, to be chopped up into hams and sides of bacon. My job was to salt the meat, in the pantry at the back. I used to mix brown sugar with the salt, it gives home-cured bacon a really nice flavour. It makes it really tasty.

One season that every Dalesman over sixty will never forget was the arctic winter of 1947, a siege of snow that blanketed the Dales for weeks on end, blotting out the walls and even whole trees – a vast, eerie whiteness. It followed a hot, dry summer, so dry that hay was scarce and expensive. Worse, the blizzard came late, when the sheep were starting to lamb and needed their feed. And few farms then owned heavy equipment to move the snow. Edith's memory of those awful weeks must echo those of many others.

All the food in the house was used up, and all the cow-cake and all the hay. We hardly had a thing, and the poor sheep were out there in the snow, almost frozen, so cold they could hardly move. Our postman managed to make his way to the door every four days or so. He'd arrive on foot and, it made me laugh, he'd be clothed from head to foot in brown paper, just as though he was a parcel himself – especially as he was such a little chap. He said it kept him warm. He'd come into the sitting-room to unwrap himself, and before he went out again he'd stick some fresh, dry sheets on. One morning he told us he'd heard that the RAF were going to drop some food, for us and the animals. He told us to lay out some sacks on the snow in the form of a cross, and when you hear the plane coming, to set fire to it to make a column of smoke. Well, they came in low, low enough to frighten the children, and down came the loads like bombs. First the groceries, all spread out along the path, then more planes with bales of hay that burst open when they hit the ground. We had to dig it out of the snow and carry it to the barn

The hardships of a Yorkshire winter, rescuing sheep
from deep snow-drifts.
OVERLEAF Outbarns in Wensleydale among a tracery of
melting snow.

in our arms. Even so, that winter was a disaster. We had 400 sheep at that time, and I think we buried 120 of them in a big pit in the corner of the field. And we had 22 calves, all skin and bone. There's never been another winter like that one, and I hope there never will be.

When the snows melt and the spring sunshine begins to warm the land, the main crop – indeed, almost the only crop – starts to colour the valley: grass. Until the 1950s, most of this grass crop was natural and was well-mixed with wild flowers. It produced one of the glories of the Dales – the hay-meadows, the hay which fed the sheep and cattle during the winter. The making and storage of hay is the imperative behind the valley stonescape of barns and walls, enclosing the delicious, scented meads. An old hay-meadow, one that may never have felt the bite of the plough, will be shot through with purple cranesbills and burnets, crimson clovers, yellow hay-rattles and trefoils and white moon-daisies. Others may be so bright with buttercups that one would be forgiven for thinking that they were the intended crop. They aren't, of course. Growing grass for hay (and, once the hay is cut, for after-grazing) is an unsentimental business involving, at least before the tractor took over, back-breaking work for somebody. The flowers were there because of biology, not because they were wanted, though many farmers believe that a leavening of flowers 'sweetens' the hay and produces tastier beef and lamb. So long as the fields were cut late and fertilized with nothing more than manure, the flowers were a fact of life – and a banquet of nectar for bees and butterflies during the late spring and early summer. Today, alas, many of the old flower-meadows are gone. Most still grow grass, and hardly any have been ploughed. But it is just grass now, uniform green, without wild colour. It is nitrate fertilizer from a sack coupled with improved drainage that has done the trick, hence the new name for green of a particular, bilious hue: 'Fison's Green'. In Fison's Green meadows the grass grows fast and early, so fast that few other plants get a look-in. And since the farmer can cut the grass several times a year while it is still green, he can make do with a much smaller acreage. He makes silage out of it, which is stored in bales of black polythene, like giant mint humbugs. Many of the stone outbarns, where the hay used to be stored, are now empty, no more useful than ruined castles.

These changes have taken place within living memory. Many Dales farmers can remember the busy weeks of haymaking which dominated the farming calendar in midsummer. It is one of those scenes, endlessly reproduced in pictures and prints, which somehow captures the heart of old England: the smocks and the billycock hats, the scythes, wooden rakes and pitchforks, the patient cart-horse with its wooden sled, the pot of cider cooling in the hedgerow, the sweet scents of drying hay and the hypnotic drone of bees. Behind the rustic charm lay a great deal of lore and skill, for it is no simple matter to cut and dry hay under Yorkshire's fickle skies. It was a matter of judging the moment when the hay was on the turn, and when the weather was in a kind mood. There is a saying in Yorkshire that if there's enough blue sky to patch a Dutchman's trousers, it's going to be a hay day. Probably every farmer had his own way of doing it. Dales farmer Gordon Falshaw remembers a whole series of operations that took place between cutting the stalks and storing them in the barn.

> I remember the days when we turned the hay by hand and then strewed it over the ground so that it could dry naturally in the sunshine. Later we got what we called a dashing machine with big spikes on the back, which was drawn along by the horse. It used to toss the hay up in the air, and you'd follow after it with your rakes, working the hay into rows. If it looked damp, you had to make these little hay cocks, then give them a shake with a fork next day. It was a hell of a procedure, really. It seemed to take ages, and we must have had about six times the acreage for hay compared with what we have today.

After the hay was dry, it was brought to one of the stone outbarns that are still scattered throughout the Dales. This, too, was a finicky business – hay is awkward stuff to handle and lift, and all kinds of ingenious tools to accommodate it were made by the village joiner. You could tell where you were in the Dales by the shape of the hay-sweep, a kind of horse-drawn rake. Marie Hartley, the local historian, remembers the Swaledale sweep as 'a little triangular thing. In Teesdale they used what was called a wing-sweep, while Wensleydale sweeps had bit handles and a long cross-bar of wood with prongs sticking out.' Then there were the hay-sledges used to carry the hay across level ground, a broad, flat sledge made up of twin wooden runners with laths laid across it. And finally, as Marie remembers:

> The hay was thrown into the barn through a hole. Outside there was a man, 'forking up,' as it was called, while inside there was a second person ready to stamp it down before the next lot came in. That was a nasty job. It gets very hot,

and occasionally an owl would fly out at you. After an hour or two of stamping and jumping about, they came out with red faces, I can tell you!

Nor was even that the end of it. After haymaking, the fields had to be manured, and that meant more horse journeys to and from the farmyard with cartloads of dung to be spread out with a 'muck fork'. About half a field a day was a good rate of mucking. The fields were not, then, empty spaces; this was still the timeless old England of *Piers Plowman*: 'a somer season whan soft was the sonne', 'a faire felde ful of folke … Worching and wandryng as the world asketh.'

It was because haymaking was so time-consuming and labour-intensive that some farmers would hire gangs of labourers at harvest-time. And the labourers came from Ireland, from as far away as County Mayo on the wind-kissed rim of the Atlantic. They were jokingly called the July Barbers, the men who 'shaved' the fields once a year with their scythes. They arrived in the villages each year in June, ready to barter their labour in true country fashion: 'with a nod and a wink, a bargain struck, a handshake and the chink of silver to drink the man's health.' Gordon Falshaw remembers the procedure.

You usually picked the same man, if he was a good worker. They used to bed down in a back room or outbuilding which was sometimes called the Irishmen's Room. They weren't 'at home' very often, though, as, after the day's work, they were always ready for a long session in the pub, drinking beer and smoking their pipes. There were some real old, good old characters among them, and they were very hard workers. They combed through the hay-field in a row, six or eight of them, raking or turning it, and loading the hay on to carts. If it rained during haymaking they used to top the thistles or chop the bracken. They were out with their scythes in all weathers, even when it was chucking it down. We usually hired them for the month, and then they moved on, perhaps to another farm over the hill.

Although they were out in the fields and the fellside all week, the Irish never worked on Sundays. But 'they all liked a glass of beer. They soon got to know the village people, and they really livened up an evening with their songs. But when the tractors came along in the early 1950s, the times changed and they were no longer needed. We miss them quite a lot, really.'

Bringing the dry hay to the barn using a Swaledale-style
sweep sometime during the 1930s.

While a few Dales farmers still make hay, the survival of the remaining flower-
fields owes much more to tourism and nature conservation than to economic
necessity. Bluntly, they benefit the visitor, not the farmer, and it is the taxpayer
who now foots the bill for them, through one scheme or another. But the farmer
can hardly be blamed for the loss of beauty, for the spread of Fison's Green. Mike
Harding, for one, sympathizes with his dilemma.

Farmers have been told to produce more, and that's what they've done. I feel
sorry for them more than anything else, because they hardly know where they're
coming from, half the time. They're told to produce more and then to produce
less; encouraged to buy more cows, then told they've lost their milk quota.
Caught between the Ministry of Agriculture on the one hand and the National

Park on the other, they're somehow expected to find a balance between pro-ducing and conserving. It's difficult.

Traditional hay-meadows were the opposite of the uniform level of green which seems to be the goal of the agriculture industry. They were full of undrained hollows, little winding streams and seepages, tussocks of coarse grass and rush. They were full of insects, food for the nestling birds and, since they were not mown until July, there was time for curlews, lapwings and other ground-nesting birds to rear their young at least to the stage where they could run away as the tractor approached. With the loss of such fields, we are losing some of the most evocative sights and sounds of the Dales. Bill Mitchell regrets this. 'One thing I feel very sad about is the absence of the dawn chorus, the choir of curlews, lapwings, redshanks, yellow wagtails. You were deafened by the sound of curlews circling and yelping when they thought their young were threatened. I remember seeing what turned out to be the last of the local corncrakes, brought to me still very much alive by the butcher's dog, which must have picked it up in the meadow.' Roger Nelson adds:

> The change from hay to silage means that the lapwing doesn't really have time to complete its nest cycle. It lays its eggs in April, and they take nearly a month to hatch. That takes us into May, and last year they were chain-harrowing the ground at that time – so that meant scrambled lapwings' eggs. Those birds with enough heart would lay again, but that takes them into June when those same farmers are cutting the grass for silage. So there's another crop of lapwings gone, and by then it's too late to start again. The lapwings that survive nest on the edges of fields or further up the hill on pastureland which doesn't receive so much cultivation. Overall, though, the numbers have gone down. We still have quite a lot of lapwings in the Dales, but I meet farmers from other parts who tell me they haven't seen any for years.

The curlew – that bubbling, wailing voice of the wild – has fared better than the lapwing, partly because most pairs nest higher up on the fell. It is still the archetypal bird of the Dales; indeed, Mike Harding thinks it should replace the sheep as the symbol of the National Park. The curlew is also more adaptable, possibly more intelligent, than the lapwing. Roger Nelson has seen the parent bird shepherding its chicks out of the field as the mowing machines arrive. Thanks to its sharp eyesight, the curlew gets plenty of warning – from its look-out post it can see trouble coming from ¼ mile (0.4 kilometres) away.

There is one wild bird of the Dales which matters a great deal more than an evocative call and a thrill of coloured feathers – the red grouse. The hardiest of birds, the grouse lives on the moors all year round and never strays very far off the hill. And it is our one bird which is unique to Britain. Nowhere else in the world can you find *Lagopus lagopus scoticus*. Europhiles and spoilsports may claim that this most British of birds is no more than a race of the Continental willow ptarmigan and, biologically speaking, they may be right. But the British grouse doesn't behave like its Continental cousin. With its call like a little, angry, old man, its near-exclusive diet of heather, its useful habit of congregating together in large numbers, the red grouse is a most individual bird. It is also famously good to eat and the most challenging of moving targets. Some half a million of them are shot each year on carefully tended moorlands from Caithness to South Wales. Their density in North Yorkshire is as high as anywhere, and the grouse is an important – and scenically vital – ingredient of the Dales economy. Sir Anthony Milbank:

He is the key, the reason for the preservation of the moorland landscape. We have a kind of love affair with this bird that we shoot and kill. We worry about him all year round – something that is hard to explain to anyone who doesn't live up here and doesn't understand the way of life. The grouse is the only bird that lives on the moor all winter, that endures all the cold winds and snow and the lashing rain. Every single feather on the grouse multiplies eight times in winter. Then, come the spring, you see the old cocks with their red combs up, looking very glamorous, setting up their territories. They quite literally patrol their pitch and fight to maintain it. For a while, the noise on the moor is fantastic, when you see them tearing hell out of each other. And then, in May, they disappear completely, and you walk over the moors and think, my God, I haven't got a single grouse. A few weeks later, you might be driving along and see ten little bumblebees sitting on a tall snatch of heather, and you think what the devil are those, and then you realize you're looking at two-day-old grouse chicks. You watch their progress over the rest of the summer, growing at amazing speed. By the start of the shooting season, on the glorious 12th of August, they are already fully grown and have been flying for some time. Once they've been shot at, the grouse grow wilder, and they group together in packs for protection. They realize instinctively that their

best chance of survival is to fly over the guns in a great cloud of birds. And, of course, the moment they see a Land Rover, or a beater's flag, they're off in a flash to the far side of the moor. So, as the shooting season gets on, it becomes more and more difficult to drive them. We normally finish in October – having shot out the surplus, but leaving the basic breeding stock – unless you have had an exceptional year, when you might go on to the end of the season on 10 December.

Behind the shooting there is a full year of moorland maintenance: keeping predators, like crows and foxes, down, burning the heather to produce a mosaic of different ages, spraying the invading bracken, repairing your shooting box, and the walls and Land Rover tracks. That is where much of the money goes. The more you can make from the shooting, the more you can plough back into the management of the moor and the maintenance of the estate. So the grouse is the key; and the other birds and wildlife that use the moors owe their livelihoods to him.

The beautiful purpling moors above the Dales do indeed owe their survival to the large sporting estates of North Yorkshire and Durham. Although heather may

ABOVE A cock red grouse.
LEFT A curlew near its nest site in the spring,
and looking alert for trouble.

seem like the wildest of wild plants, these huge stands of dense, flowering heather need careful tending. And though there may appear to be plenty of it still, English heather moorland has declined by as much as 40 per cent since the war. The place where Sir Anthony Milbank bagged his first grouse is now pasture, with not a sprig of heather visible for half a mile. The main enemy is the sheep. There are far more grazing the high moors today than there were fifty years ago, and their effect can be seen in the gradual displacement of the purple mantle by the advancing carpet of green. Much of the North Pennines is common land, where the grazing is beyond the control of the landlord or anybody else. It is only on the privately owned moors that the future of heather – and grouse – seems reasonably secure.

Grouse-shooting, the very pinnacle of field sports activities, has always been accompanied by ceremony. Nowadays, most grouse moors are let to shooting syndicates, but in more leisured times their owners could afford to keep the moor for themselves and their friends. Lord Peel remembers the 'great trek' that his family and retainers took from Lancashire to Gunnerside Lodge in Swaledale each August at the start of the shooting season.

My father used to talk about it for weeks – no, months – in advance. He called it the gathering of the clansmen, all his friends from different parts of Britain. And indeed from abroad – I remember Sir Humphrey Gibbs coming over when he was Governor-General of Rhodesia. It was a great occasion, this entourage of vehicles, my father at the head with his chauffeur, my brother and myself next, with the luggage, and a third one following behind with the staff. Though it was only 47 miles [76 kilometres], you'd think we were crossing India. Pat Fox, who looked after the lodge for us, would be on the terrace looking down the valley to see the trekkers approaching, and we'd draw up in grand style amid a great bustle – it was always a big occasion.

The shooting was taken very seriously, especially when you arrived at the butts. It was a masculine occasion – the guns, as the marksmen are known, were not allowed to bring their wives, although, as a great concession, the landlord might make an exception for his own family. Lord Peel always knew that someone was dreadfully ill if his wife turned up with him – it meant she was there to stop him keeling over in his grouse butt. It was a highly organized event, right down to the last detail of the substantial hamper. The guns in their shooting garb and polished shoes were the immaculate core of a bustle of dogs, and beaters with their sticks and flags, and local farmers who turned up to help. In those days there might also be ponies with pannier baskets, for there could be a long walk through the heather out to the butts. The more infirm members of the party might be put on horse-back. Lord Peel remembers that one of them was called Mr Rider, and he, of course, fell off. 'My brother thought it incredibly funny that Mr Rider should have fallen off a horse. It's funny, isn't it, the things that stick in your memory?'

In many ways, the scene has not changed much, though the parties now travel by Range Rover, and there is seldom far to walk. Tweeds and plus-fours are still *de rigueur* and the grouse are no easier to hit. The accommodation, however, is considerably less spartan. Many of the shooting parties on the Duke of Devonshire's Bolton Abbey estate stay at the Devonshire Arms Hotel, while at Gunnerside Lodge modern comforts have replaced the cold showers, oil lamps and bare linoleum from the days of Lord Peel's father.

Perhaps the greatest change has been in the role of the gamekeeper, the *sine qua non* of the sporting estate. The old-style keeper, the sworn enemy of everything toothed and clawed, has all but disappeared. Few modern gamekeepers maintain

A shooting party on a Yorkshire grouse moor in 1931.

gibbets – those dangling rows of vermin and possible vermin strung up on the fence for inspection and a tip. A modern keeper is more of an estate manager, concerned as much with maintaining the whole habitat as with the grouse and its predators. Kevin Drummond compares his work with that of a gardener. 'A 5000-acre [2000-hectare] garden of heather and berries. I class as the weeds the predators that prey on the grouse and other species that use the moor. Gardening the moor means caring for the heather, producing the tender, young flowering heather by burning in a rotation – otherwise we'd end up with just the old gnarled kind we call a bog brush.'

Unlike the gamekeepers of old, Kevin Drummond actually welcomes the little merlin, our smallest bird of prey, on his grouse moor.

When I came here in the 1970s, you never saw a peregrine, or a moor owl or a merlin. The reason wasn't the keeper – it was the scientific boffins that were responsible, with their pesticides and insecticides. Then, around 1980, a merlin

ABOVE A cock merlin on its moorland nest –
'a natural gamekeeper'.
LEFT An adult roe buck in his red-brown summer coat.

came back. I hadn't realized the good they can do until I watched this little jack merlin chase off a couple of carrion crows. And, I thought, there's a little keeper in the making. Because he wasn't just protecting his own nest, but also those of three grouse, two curlews, an oystercatcher and a lapwing. Since then we've had more merlins moving in, dotted about the moors. I call them my little sentries – they're doing no harm to the grouse, and it's nice to think that you've got somebody else helping you, out there on the moor.

Grouse-shooting in the Dales has changed from an aristocratic leisure pursuit to a commercial business, enabling landowners like Lord Peel to plough back income

143

into improving the stock of grouse and restoring areas of damaged heather. It is essentially a long-term investment in the future of moorland. Could the moors survive without it? Sir Anthony Milbank is doubtful.

> I think there probably is an alternative – if you use large amounts of taxpayers' money and many government agencies, and with a lot of effort, including the reform of the CAP, you might save the heather habitat. But I doubt whether you'd have any birds to live there. That comes from management, and for that you need income from the grouse. And the love of it. My grandfather would have had forty fits if he'd known I'd gone into this commercial shooting business. But without it, it would be hard to maintain the moors and their stocks of grouse.
>
> In my heart of hearts, I do worry about the future of shooting. The social trend is against it, away from killing. When the king felt it was no longer necessary to hunt deer in his forests, the forests soon disappeared. I feel the same way about the grouse moors. I really worry about the future of a lot of moorland birds. My fellow moor owners will kill me for saying that.

Those who have lived in the Dales since the 1940s have seen great changes, as profound in their effects as anywhere in England, though perhaps in less obvious ways. Much of the back-break has gone out of farming, but the weather, especially the long winters, has not changed. Not long ago, shepherds would walk up the fell on their own two feet, with dog and stick. Now most own four-wheel quad bikes that can zoom about on the tops without leaving any surface marks (though some sheepdogs refuse to ride on them). The sheep are shaved by machine, and so is the grass. Fewer, many many fewer, people work on the land. The internal combustion engine has changed all that. It has brought many benefits, but stresses also as Ron Metcalfe explains: 'There used to be a lot more time in the day than there is now. The pace of life has increased. The motor car allows us to get to town easily. But there are far too many cars on the road now. You can't move sheep and cattle on the roads as easily as our fathers could; and some drivers don't know what to do when the road is full of livestock. Instead we have to take them to market in trucks, at the risk of injuries. It's grand that visitors can come and appreciate the Dales, but on some days it gets a bit much.' Nor are the roads the ideal cycling territory that they were. Many cyclists now head for the hills and the rough country on their mountain bikes.

The National Park has preserved many a fine farmstead and barn, and provides an excellent service to the visitor with its footpaths and car parks, its centres and booklets. The role of National Park wardens is a delicate one, since the Park is not universally popular, and the Commission's powers are circumscribed by law and landlessness. Many visitors fail to realize that virtually all the Yorkshire Dales are still private land. Mike Harding is critical about some aspects of the Park: their failure, for example, to do much about the large-scale quarrying operations that scar the landscape or the misery of low-flying military aircraft. 'They're good at telling people not to change the shape of their windows or restricting the size of signs, but not so good at stopping golf courses being built or preventing the decline of the lapwing. I don't think the Park staff have a good enough relationship with local people yet. The latter still feel the Park has been imposed on them.' The essential contradiction of our National Parks was summed up in a phrase by one of their own Commissioners: 'solitude for the masses'. Who has the prior claim, the visitor from the towns and cities, or the people who work the land and live in the landscape? Many farmers, like Gordon Falshaw, are now paid not to produce anything. 'We're allowed one bag of fertilizer per acre [0.4 hectare], and they seem to want us to go back to where we were fifty years ago. I've been fortunate in being able to convert a barn into a self-catering hostel, and so make some alternative income that way. I'm sure it's a damn sight easier than mucking cows out. But I think if you come back in fifteen years' time you'll find us all walking round with a National Park warden's badge on our sleeves.'

In the modern world where everything seems to have its price, places like the Dales have provided at the very least an incalculable store of one commodity that cannot be weighed in money and therefore tends to be undervalued – simple human happiness. Pleasure in being within a wonderful landscape is something that is shared by resident and incomer alike. No one expressed this better than Mike Harding, who discovered the Dales for the first time at the age of thirteen. 'I'd saved three pounds ten shillings from my newspaper round, and me and my mate Dave cycled there with our food in a gas mask bag. It was the first time I'd ever seen a cow. I lived by the ICI dye works in Manchester, where a yellow fella would go past, and a green dog would chase a purple cat. Imagine suddenly finding a landscape like this with streams and rivers and open spaces and green everywhere. The smell of the air instead of the factory chimney. To me that was paradise on earth.'

THE MIGHTY RIVER Tweed rises, it is said, on the same hill as the Clyde and the Annan. Though not a dramatic hill, and certainly no mountain, Tweedsmuir is the great watershed of southern Scotland, a kind of aquatic roundabout: the Clyde beginning its westward race to Glasgow; the Annan slipping away southwards, a silver pencil line in the beautiful dale that emerges in the Solway Firth; and the Tweed, bubbling through cushions of moss and rippling over gravel to begin its long journey to the North Sea. The Tweed is the life-blood of the Borders. Its arterial flow links lonely castles and ruined abbeys, surges between the hills, and broadens into weed-winding banks as it is joined by other waters, draining the out-spread limbs and fingers of the Border country. To stress its dominant place in the scenery, only the Tweed, and its tributary the Teviot, are dignified by the name of 'river'. The other flows, on the Scottish side at least, are named 'waters', as if they know their place. They are the subalterns and minions of the great river, the Tweoda of the ancient Saxons, possibly the Teva of the Roman cartographer, a name that paid homage to this powerful swell of water.

Looking across the Tweed near the attractive Border
town of Peebles.

The Tweed serves the Borders in many ways, both direct and indirect. The current of the Tweed and its minions drove the great wheels of the textile mills, the source of the wealth of Galashiels, Selkirk, Innerleithen and other Borders townships. In the days before the railways, the Tweed was also the main highway through the region, and it is said that people made their way to Edinburgh in summer along the dry bed of the Gala. The river washed the meadows of farmsteads and abbeys, and produced the fish for Lenten suppers. For most Border homes, the sight of boats and the sound of surging water were never far away.

Most people, though, will associate the River Tweed with one thing above all – with the king of the fish, the salmon, the finny basis of an entire river economy. In its quest for the gravelly spawning grounds far away among the hills, the salmon had to run the gauntlet of boats, nets and fly rods. There were the nets of offshore boats and the staked nets on the beach near Goswick. There were the little coble boats along the river, each with its semicircular curtain of drift net with a man at either end. And, of course, there were the coloured flies skipping or floating above the river, each one concealing a hook and a line that connected with the man standing patiently in mid-stream. The salmon was a way of life for boatmen and gillies, netsmen, bailiffs and poachers, as well as the finest imaginable sport for the privileged few.

You have to make a special effort to find and explore the land of the Tweed, and ignore the magnetic tug of Edinburgh and the Highlands. The Borders have always been a secluded region, locked away among the hills. In the mid-nineteenth century the area seemed to open up in a flurry of road- and railway-building. Today, though, the railways have closed down and the main roads either bypass the area or strike briskly through it, without offering many inducements to halt. The Borders have once again become one of the quietest, emptiest parts of Britain outside the Highlands. They appeal most to visitors with a sense of adventure, to those who love riding among the hills, fishing the rivers or roaming in search of ruined castles and abbeys. To enjoy the Borders you need to relax into a slower tempo of life, forget about timetables and deadlines, and allow yourself to wander, to linger in the elegant town squares and set off on foot or horseback to probe the secrets of this or that inviting valley.

There is a hint of enchantment in the Borders, which inspired many of the works of Sir Walter Scott and his contemporary, James Hogg, the poet known as the 'Ettrick Shepherd'. The writer and novelist, Elizabeth Taylor, finds a particular magic in the landscape of the Eildons, in a peculiar saucer of land crowned in the centre by three strange, conical hills.

> No matter where you are, your eyes are drawn to them. They say that King Arthur sleeps there with his knights, awaiting the nation's call. And there's the well-known story of Thomas the Rhymer who went up into the hills one day and met the Queen of the Fairies. He stayed among the fairies for what he thought were seven days, but on his return found he'd been away for seven years. I'm sure that that is an allegory of life in the Borders. Time slides past here; you can be away for a long time, then take up the threads where you left them as if you'd never been away.

The Borders landowner, the Duke of Buccleuch, remembers one occasion when it seemed as though an Eildon legend was coming true before his eyes.

> I was standing with my back to Little Eildon and explaining to a party of visitors how, when Scotland is threatened by invasion, men on horseback will appear from a crack in the hillside to ride to the nation's defence. The sun was setting behind me as I told them this, and suddenly their expressions changed. They all looked quite horror-struck and seemed to freeze. I couldn't think what was the matter, so I turned round and, lo and behold, there indeed was a troop of horsemen appearing to emerge from the hill. It soon became clear that it was only the local pony trekking brigade. But for a moment I think my party really thought that this was the real thing.

The Borders are still an area of large estates and tenanted farms – it is said that there are more dukes per square mile here than in any other part of Britain. Social change seems slower than in many areas, and time-honoured habits of deference and mutual obligation remain. Elizabeth Taylor notices a certain Borders fatalism – what will be will be – and a sense that our lives are ruled by a nameless 'they'. 'They' are not necessarily the laird, or the local authority, or even the government. Elizabeth found this out when she tried to organize a petition to save the local

OVERLEAF Scott's View, looking towards the
Eildon hills, and in the far distance the hills that give birth
to the Tweed.

railway bridge from demolition. 'Everyone said, "Oh, you canna do that." If *they* said it had to come down, that was that. I said it's not *their* bridge, it's *our* bridge, but they'd shake their heads. Though in the end I did get more than 4000 signatures, and we did save the bridge.'

Although the strict social hierarchies of previous generations are rapidly dissolving, a time-honoured social ritual still remains. Elizabeth recalls the elaborately graded signals with which her father's groom, Hughie, would greet participants at the hunt.

'To a duke or an earl, he would always doff his black bowler. That was the only time we ever saw his hair – black with a little curl plastered on his forehead. The gentry would get a more perfunctory tilting of the bowler. He would oblige the proprietor farmer with a touch of the whip to the brim of his hat, and a smart "Good morning to you". For anyone else, it was just a nod and a "Good morning", and some were ignored altogether.'

This was not blind snobbery but a more or less unconscious observance of social convention, instilled in rural families almost from birth. It was in the way of things. History was, like the river, a continuing stream. You went with the current. Tom Arres, one-time mole-catcher and dry-stone diker, explains the intricate social hierarchy:

You had the laird, who owned the land and was almost all-powerful. He lets his farm land to tenants, who used to employ farm workers, though there aren't many of those left now. But there was more to it than that: there were two grades of farmer, the gentleman farmer and the working farmer. Everybody thought themselves a cut above somebody else, you see. There were even two different kinds of cattleman. The one who looked after a pedigree herd called himself a herdsman, and was socially superior to the byreman who looked after the estate's non-pedigree cattle.

Perhaps it was the existence of a fixed, if unwritten, set of social rules that gave the Borderers their marvellously relaxed attitude to life. Elizabeth Taylor speaks of the sense of freedom and openness that matches and reflects the landscape. 'People here are friendly and tolerant. Once they have the measure of you and you're accepted, they place you, and there you stay. You can be as eccentric as you like – in fact, it's almost encouraged.' Mind you, unless you were born and brought up here, you will never be a paid-up native Borderer, as Ronnie Rose found. 'I moved here twenty-five years ago, and am involved in the church and the guild, and get on tremendously well with the local farmers. They're all very nice to me, and it's all very friendly. But you're still an incomer.'

A love of the open, free-roaming landscape of river and hill is obvious in every Borderer we spoke to. For Andrew Hepburne-Scott it began in his childhood, when the whole family would take off on horseback – for the Borders are riding country, perhaps Britain's nearest approach to Calgary or the High Chaparral.

> It was always fun riding out on to the hill. There were no gates or fences there, just these wide open, heather-covered spaces. One came on to farms way out above the valley, and shepherds working their sheep in the stell [an enclosure]; the feeling that one could ride for miles and miles across limitless space, and the sense of freedom it gave you.

For Elizabeth Taylor, Border rides framed her early intimacy with the landscape and its wildlife.

> One of the good things about doing so much riding as a child was that we really got to know the countryside. We saw it in all its moods, in all weathers. It was a real feeling of belonging to the landscape. We saw so many things. Little valleys coated with bluebells, wild hyacinths, in the spring. And the high moors above the Lauder with hundreds of lapwings calling. It is very much part of my memories, the birds and the flowers. When I returned here as an adult, I'd turn a corner and see a fence or a gate, and think: I *know* that field, I've ridden across it and I know where it goes on the other side. That feeling moved me to tears.

Nowhere is the Borders love of riding and roaming more visible than in the celebrated Common Ridings, held by a number of towns each year in early summer. The Ridings are a form of 'beating the bounds', and are conducted with full ceremony. At Selkirk, the riders head forth out of the town square with the town band playing, in a great troop of horses that recalls the wild old days of Border raiding parties and the flower of Scotland riding to death and glory at Flodden Field. At Galashiels, the procession is more stately, with the flutter of banners and the drone of the pipes. The arms of the Burgh are carried by the 'braw lad' from the

153

The crossing of the Tweed at Braw Lad's Gathering
at Galashiels, one of the famous Common Ridings of the
Border townships.

town war memorial, down the Selkirk road and across the river to Abbotsford for a glass of wine and a complimentary exchange of roses with the descendants of Sir Walter Scott. The climactic moment is the crossing of the Tweed, on horseback, cantering down to the river in great style, banners waving, and into the shallows with a tremendous splashing, a sight to stir the dormant Border reiver in us all. On their return, the lad's partner, the 'braw lass', presents red and white roses to signify the Union of the Crowns of Scotland and England. In the old days, the procession was the climax to a whole week of fun, but latterday spoilsports have restricted the Braw Lad's Gathering to a single day.

The original purpose of the Ridings was to inspect the common pastures of the town, to check for illegal encroachments and to ensure that everything was as it should be. Such was the spread of land involved that it took the best part of a day on horseback to circumnavigate the boundary. That the Ridings continue today in such style, with such enthusiastic participation, is a tribute to the immense civic pride of these isolated Border towns. And with pride, of course, goes strong rivalry. You can still find people who will claim that a day away from Hawick is a day wasted, or meet a Selkirk man who wouldn't be seen dead in Hawick, or Galashiels either, for that matter. At one time it would have caused a scandal for a lass from one town to marry a lad from another – a theme for Sir Walter Scott, perhaps. Much of this ancient feeling is sublimated today in rugby matches, which are watched and played here with every bit as much passion and dedication as in South Wales. Melrose claims that the fast seven-a-side rugby, now played all over the Borders, originated there. Other towns, of course, dispute this.

What nearly all of these towns have in common is the original basis of their wealth: wool, shorn from hill sheep. Like the salmon, the woollen industry depended originally on the river, in this case on the current of the water to power the factory wheels. The progress from a sheep to knitwear took in a large slice of the Borders economy, from shepherd to dyers and weavers and cottagers, to the market and the shop. In the Borders, the sheep is a very familiar object. Miss Brown, a village schoolteacher, tells a nice story of how a schools inspector once pinned a picture of a sheep to the blackboard and asked the young children to name it. There was a pause while the children scratched their heads and a whispered discussion went on between the desks. Finally, somewhat disappointed, the inspector said, 'Well, it's a sheep. Don't you know that?' Of course they knew what a sheep was. The point at issue was whether the animal was a Border blackface or one of the newer cross-breeds.

The trade in wool from the Borders, traditionally of the finest quality, financed the building of abbeys at Melrose, Jedburgh, Kelso and Dryburgh, still magnificent in their ruinous state near the banks of the river. More modest, but still quite grand, are the mansions of the mill owners of the Industrial Age, baronial piles outside the town, designed by French architects and decorated by Italian plasterers. It was the textile mills that brought surfaced roads and railways to the Borders, and opened the area up to trade and outside influence. What they made was tweed cloth which is, incidentally, nothing to do with the river of that name; this tweed is a variation of 'tweel' or twill – apparently the result of a mistake by a London clothmaker who mistakenly wrote a 'd' for an 'l' when ordering tweel.

The booming mill towns changed the social fabric of the region, producing wage workers as well as shepherds and cottagers, and a new kind of life, regulated by the factory whistle and the clatter of machinery. What was unusual was that many of the new jobs were taken by women. As Elizabeth Taylor emphasizes: 'As wage-earners they became very independent, almost feminist in their views. Many kept their maiden names. I remember how they organized bus parties and went on what they called mystery tours, arriving back late at night, singing raucously.'

Another vein of early feminism was developing on rural land. While the carding machines rattled, while Hawick turned out quality woollen socks and stockings, while Galashiels produced twin-sets by the ton, the rhythm of life in the surrounding country was governed by social position, the daily routine and the calendar. Right up to the Second World War, the bottom rung in the land hierarchy was occupied by a kind of indentured slavery, by female farm labourers known as bondagers. The custom in which a hired man's wife, sister or daughter might be obliged to accompany him to work on the land had its origins in the farming improvements of the eighteenth century, for with them came a greater demand for cheap, landless labour. The bondager was normally obliged to work for a year, and hard work it usually was, threshing and harvesting, hoeing the turnip fields and spreading the muck. Elizabeth Taylor knew one tiny, frail old woman who had gone to the hiring-fair with her brother in search of work. 'They hoped that he would be hired as a farm worker and she as his bondager. They were always the last to be hired for, being very small, nobody thought they were up to hard work. She told me she was set to work carrying sacks of corn on her back up a ladder into the hay loft. And each one weighed more than she did. That was her first job.'

There were other stories of farmers putting bondagers between the shafts and making them pull the cart if the horse was sick. But despite the hardship of their lives, the bondagers are said to have possessed tremendous *esprit de corps,* and there were always plenty of women willing to join them – the main alternatives being the textile mills or domestic service. They worked in gangs. At the barn dances or ceilidhs you could always spot the bondager girl by the brown oval or triangle across her face where the sun had caught her between the brim of her broad hat and her woollen headscarf. Elizabeth Taylor remembers them well.

They looked marvellous. They wore a traditional costume that hadn't changed much down the years. In summertime it consisted of a wide straw or canvas

Bondagers threshing corn around 1920 – using a
traction engine and a threshing mill. The ladies on the ricks
wear the characteristic bondager headgear.

bonnet they called an Ugly, made on hoops of bamboo with a frill at the back to shade their necks. Sometimes they wore headscarves over it to keep it down. And they wore calf-length striped skirts, big sacking aprons and coloured cotton blouses; dark lisle stockings and strong men's boots. When it was muddy they made ropes out of straw and wound them round and round their legs. In winter the Ugly was replaced by a wonderful black lacquered hat, like a great saucer with a flat brim and wound round with coloured cotton, all tied down with a scarf. Altogether it was a most glamorous 'costume'. It was quite a sight when you saw a group of them coming along the road. And the younger women, especially, always kept themselves smart.

Another way of earning a living was to learn one or more necessary rural skills and hire yourself out to the local farms. In his time, Tom Arres has been a mole-trapper, a shepherd and a dry-stone diker, as the builders of stone walls are known north of the Border. He started off, however, as a rat-catcher, at the rate of a penny a tail. 'I had to hand the tails in to the farm steward at the end of the month – you cut them off to prove you'd killed the rat. But this old steward always said, "No, no, laddie, I'm not going to count 'em, I'll take your word for it." Well, I was proud that he trusted me, but after a while it dawned on me what ailed him. It was the smell of the tails in the box – it was fit to blow the lid off, and that's why he didn't want to count them.'

Rat-catching wasn't a bad living. By catching seventy rats a week, using simple snares and spring sticks, Tom earned six shillings, which was almost as much as an apprentice blacksmith or joiner. Even so, rat-catching has its social limitations and he decided to move on, working with the bondagers for a while, before specializing in mole-trapping as a winter activity. 'As a boy I was fascinated by mole traps, so I started killing moles in the bad months in winter when it was getting miserable for diking.' Setting up your wares was easy. 'You just hang up your dead moles in a prominent public place, like a roadside fence. Then along comes a farmer with a bad mole problem, and he hires you and tells his neighbours, and the word just gets around, you know. I never had to advertise.' But, it seems, the traditional mole-catcher's gibbet is no longer acceptable to visitors. The Douglas-Homes, whose family seat The Hirsel is near Coldstream, had to have Tom's moles taken down after receiving complaints. Caroline Douglas-Home explains that 'we were getting letters from some of our visitors saying this was barbaric, and it wasn't what they came to the countryside to see, this row of little skinny, dead, dried-up moles. It was the same with the keeper's "larder", with all the hoodies [crows] and weasels hung up on the fence. We've had to stop that, too.'

And amen to that, some might say, but Tom Arres' gibbeted moles didn't seem to offend the people who actually live in the Borders. As he puts it, 'It seems to me that the "crime" is in killing the mole in the first place, not in what you do with the carcass afterwards.'

The Douglas-Homes are among the great Border magnates, descendants of the Douglases and Homes whose names run like a scarlet ribbon through the turbulent history of the Borders. The family seat, The Hirsel, stands by the Tweed at one of the places where the river forms the border between Scotland and

Casting a salmon fly near Abbotsford.

England. The house and its grounds are open to the public, and are refreshingly free of the more blatant attempts to part the visitor with his money. In keeping with its setting – a level of trees and parkland around the river and the swell of hills on both horizons – The Hirsel is a haven of peace and quiet. Unlike some estates, the family maintain a fishing beat on the river for part of the season. Caroline Douglas-Home remembers the restorative effect of the river on her late father, the former Prime Minister. 'He absolutely adored it. He would come home off the night-sleeper early on Saturday morning, looking grey and drawn, but he'd be on the river as soon as breakfast was over, whatever the weather. By lunchtime, he was a changed man, ruddy-faced and full of life, after a morning's fishing. One of his greatest pleasures was to help his friends catch their first salmon.'

What is it about fishing that quietly removes the burdens of work and high office and produces a feeling of inner peace? Whatever the answer is, each individual experiences it in a different way. To Caroline, it is a matter of complete immersion in the life of the river.

When I'm on the river I'm completely absorbed by what the fly is doing, or whether there's likely to be a fish behind that ripple, or that particular stone. You are immersed in what you're doing, but at the same time you have half an eye for the surroundings, the ducks or cormorants, trout rising, salmon jumping. It's a marvellous switch-off from life's hectic pace.

For Wattie Burns, a celebrated boatman, 'Every day on the river is different. You can fish for hours, and nothing much happens. Your attention wanders, and you're thinking about something else, and then, bang, he's hooked, and suddenly it's all excitement. It happens so quickly, this change from tranquillity to wild threshing about, fish jumping everywhere, falling about. But that's the challenge of salmon-fishing: the uncertainty.' Jake Harvey, who looks after a fishing syndicate on the river, believes it lies partly in the anticipation. 'Whenever I go out fishing, I'm like the wee laddie getting everything ready, looking forward to the day out. Once you're on the river, though, it's very relaxing. You're concentrating very much on trying to catch a fish, but at the same time there's the movement and sound of the river, the mood of the weather, the sounds of nature, you know. It's a wonderful feeling.' Added to which, there is what might be called the *après*-fish, the shared joke with the boatman, the fishing talk at the bar, the good food and fresh air. The curative effect of fly-fishing seems to lie in this transcendent mixture of excitement and refreshment; it may be one of the few activities where it is possible to be both exhilarated and relaxed at the same time.

Then there is the mystique of the bait, the fishing fly, with its hundreds of coloured variations and romantic names like Greendrake, Halford's Welshman's Button, Pale Evening Spinner, Iron Blue Dun. Some of the best-known fly-dressers for salmon lived by the Tweed, like James Wright and son, inventors of the Durham Ranger, the Silver Doctor and the Garry Dog, which is said to be based on the hairs plucked from the local minister's yellow Labrador of that name. One of the heirs to this tradition is Wattie Burns, inventor of the fabled Wattie's White Shrimp, reputed to be 'a real killer'. Wattie himself is more modest about its power.

> It's a variation of an old shrimp fly, tied with hair rather than feather, as the right kind of feather is hard to come by now. It's got what I like in a fly, a long tail and a ling that flexes and pulses in the river. It's very basic, but it attracts the salmon, and that's the important thing.
>
> People say salmon flies are an art in themselves. They got more and more gaudy in the nineteenth century, though some of the traditionalists on the Tweed preferred the older kind, calling the new ones 'fish frights'. But the best fly is the one you have faith in. In truth, the salmon isn't that fussy. If he's in the right mood, he'll take what you give him.

And when he does, you have that moment you have been waiting for; as one fisherman, David Hodgkiss, describes it: 'That first moment of contact, when you're in touch with a wild creature. Sometimes they take it very quietly, almost like a leaf or a bit of weed touching the fly. At other times you get a really savage take, and that's the moment we fish for.'

The salmon enter the river with just one idea in mind: to get as far upstream as they can, to spawn in the shallow gravel reaches in the headwaters high up among the hills. Mature salmon never feed in freshwater and live for months on their reserves of body fat and muscle. By the time they reach the spawning ground, they may have been in the river for several months. Spawning may be among the last acts of their lives. The hen fish cuts a trough called a redd with her tail. While she huddles down and lays her eggs in the redd, the cock fish swims alongside and fertilizes the eggs with his 'milt'. Having performed these extraordinary contortions on empty stomachs the salmon then depart downstream. But, as every reader of Henry Williamson's *Salar the Salmon* will know, they are unlikely to return to the sea. Death is their lot, as their last reserves of energy seep away and fungus or predators seize their opportunity.

The young fish, known as elvins or fry, hatch out after a few months. After their yolk sac is consumed, they become parr, feeding actively in the river, and living much as young trout do, on insects and worms. Depending on how well they feed, after two to four years, the salmon parr shed their old drab scales and grow a new coat of shimmering silver. The parr has become a smolt. Some smolts will congregate and leave the river for the open sea. There they become salmon. Those that don't go, or return after a year at sea, are called grilse. These seldom swim far offshore and never reach a great size. The really big salmon have lived in the sea for several years, and the longer they are there the bigger they grow. So the 20–40-pounders (9–18 kilograms) are sea fish that are fully mature, or that have fed particularly well. Either way, they will be the canniest fish in the river when they eventually return to their birthplace to spawn and die.

The salmon-fishing season ends in November and begins again in February, when it can be so cold that the water freezes on your rod and numbs your mittened fingers. But the best fishing depends on the seasonal run of salmon, and on securing one of the really good beats, like 'the marvellous deep pool beneath the walls of Roxburgh Castle'. The Tweed used to be what is known as a spring river, but in the last quarter-century the biggest runs have appeared in the autumn. And, because of over-fishing at sea, the runs are smaller, though the average size of the fish is somewhat larger. There is always a chance of catching a salmon of 30 pounds (14 kilograms) plus, the fish of a lifetime. The fishing has also become much more expensive. Most of the riparian owners on the Tweed today are fishing syndicates. Like the grouse of the Yorkshire Moors, Tweed salmon are no longer there for the sole pleasure of the country house and its guests. It is city money that pays the rents and secures the best beats now, money that helps to support the elaborate infrastructure of the salmon industry, and brings wealthy customers to the shops of Galashiels and Coldstream.

Salmon is therefore enormously important to the economy of the Borders. With the employment it gives to the boatmen, and the rents from fishing, go the hotels and guest houses, and all the infrastructure of grocers and garages and tackle shops behind them. And while the men are on the river fishing, their wives

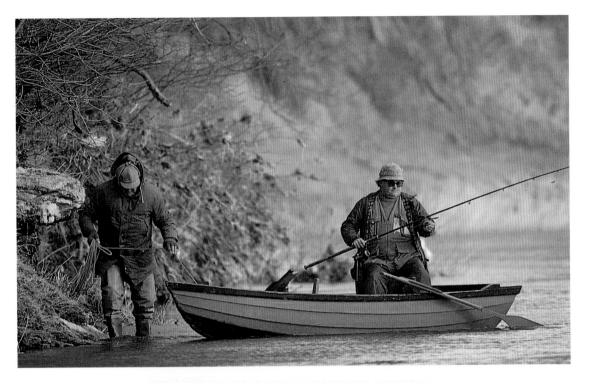

TOP A salmon fisher and his boatman on the Tweed.
ABOVE An even more expert fisher, a goosander diving
underwater to catch a young salmon.
OVERLEAF Salmon nets spread out on the bank to dry
near Tweedmouth.

visit the tweed shops and mill shops, and buy their Christmas presents. Caroline Douglas-Home knows at least one tenant who went home broke, not from her rent, but from his wife's shopping expeditions.

With so much at stake, it is not surprising that riparian owners have become concerned about over-fishing. Until recently salmon were netted in the river from the little coble boats with their curtain-like nets. When the riparian owners bought out the Berwick Salmon Fisheries in 1989 and closed down most of the fishing stations, a way of life and the practice of ancient skills came to an end. Oswald Carr, a salmon-netter since his teens, has some chilly memories.

> I've lived on the river all my life, since leaving school in 1930. We used to fish the river in two five-hour shifts, catching the ebb tide and stopping when the tide comes back in. To be successful you had to understand the currents, the way they changed from day to day, the different ways of placing your net depending on whether the water was low or high. And in cold weather you've got to reach deep down, because the fish stay near the bottom. A dark night *and* a deep fishery is a wash-out. We used to stop when it got really cold, partly because the ice cuts the net, partly because the fish stay in the sea. I remember days so cold that the blood came through your skin – we didn't wear gloves then. And in 1947 I actually walked to work across the frozen river.

Another concern is poaching, though the old-fashioned kind of poacher was as much a part of country life as the shepherd or the gillie. Back in the 1950s, many operated with the knowledge and even support of local people, who were indeed their main customers. The feeling was that the fish belonged to everybody. One contributor remembers the knock on the door after dark, and a man outside offering him a fresh salmon from a suitcase for half a crown. 'We put the big ones in the bath, to be divided up with the family next door.' Elizabeth Taylor remembers a well-known local poacher who would ride about the country on his bike with a shotgun tied to the cross-bar. 'He got slapped in gaol in Edinburgh, but we were all on his side because we felt the river belonged to anybody. If he was clever enough to catch them by hand, and not by blowing them up or poisoning them, we reckoned he deserved an award, not a gaol sentence.' It was not unknown for river bailiffs to be pelted with stones as they swept past on their steam launch.

Jake Harvey, now a successful sculptor, learned the forbidden arts of salmon-poaching in his youth, 'under the tutelage of old Urchy Beech and Tucker Hide'.

Jake Harvey

In a funny kind of way, poaching made me very conservation-conscious. It gives you a detailed understanding of fish behaviour just as much as rod-and-line fishing does.

When I was young I'd often cycle down to the river early in the morning with my rod and a pocket full of worms and maybe some salted minnows, and fish for brownies [trout] or whip-pling [sea-trout] for an hour or two. But as the sun came up, the fish tended to disappear under the stones and into the hags [boggy areas] along the bank. So I'd then put my rod away, wade out into the river and gump [poke] around with a stick to find out where they were hiding. The technique is to put your hand beneath the bank and very gently feel into all the little nooks and crannies to see if there's a fish there. It's easy to detect them from the texture of their bodies, and then you lightly run your fingers up and down their flanks, trying to per-suade them, you know, that it's just the current of the water. Then you gently close your hands around the fish, and when you feel that you've got a fairly tight grip you clasp it all of a sudden and whip it out of the water.

I know it's illegal, but at that time it was all part of childhood and growing up in the Borders. In the early 1950s there were very few televisions in the village, and we got our pleasure from roaming the hills, poaching rabbits, poaching pheasants, and coming down to the river here for a bit of fishing and a bit of gumping. We learned a lot about the countryside, as performers if you like, getting to know the natural habitat very intimately.

There were many memorable encounters and hair-raising escapes along the way. There was an on-going battle of wits between the poacher and the gamekeeper or the bailiffs. Jake remembers one night in particular.

It was just before Christmas 1964. My friend Urch and I went off to poach a pheasant for the table. It was a dark, windy evening, with cloud-cover, perfect for poaching in, and there were the usual sounds, birds flying out of the trees and rabbits scurrying around in the undergrowth. But as soon as we were in the larchwood where we hoped to bag our bird, everything went very, very quiet. We both felt it, and Urch said, 'There's something funny going on here tonight.' We had a wee chat and concluded that the gamekeeper had realized his pheasants were getting poached and that he was in there waiting for us. We decided to beat a hasty retreat. We hadn't gone far when Urch suddenly grabbed me by the shoulder, and cried, 'Jake, Jake ... look!' And I turned round, and there, about 10 feet [3 metres] in the air, was this big object the colour of a Hereford bull's eye, following us. Well, as you can imagine, we got a terrific fright and made off hell for leather across that field, back to the village and, to tell the truth, I've never poached in that wood again. To this day, I don't know how the keeper played that trick on us but, my goodness, it worked, and we've never been back.

There are more insidious threats to the king of fish than poaching. Jake Harvey believes that chemicals used on farmland as fertilizer and pesticides are leaking into the river in sufficient quantity to damage the stocks of trout and young salmon. Some years ago, he noticed that there were many fewer flies on the water. The River Board could find nothing wrong, but it later transpired that a moth-proofing agent was escaping into the river from a textile plant. Once that had been put right, the flies returned and the fishing improved. 'But for a while you couldn't dry-fly for trout, because the fish just weren't rising.'

There are occasional nasty diseases too, like when UDN – ulcerated dermal necrosis – struck the Tweed in the late 1960s and decimated the spring runs. Wattie Burns remembers the horrid sight of dead fish along the banks, all covered in white fungus 'like driven snow'. People tried to stop it spreading by burying the fish in lime pits, but after a few years the epidemic ceased of its own accord. 'Nature looked after it.'

The skills and pleasures of salmon-fishing remain eternal, despite such rumbles off-stage. The last word on the subject should be left to Wattie Burns.

The secret lies in the respect of the fisherman for his quarry. You have to love what you're doing and understand what the fish is doing. You mustn't be afraid to admit you've been beaten by the salmon – he is king, you know. There will be days when you catch two or three and think yourself the bee's knees, and then you'll catch nothing and feel the salmon has made a fool of you. We're just here to enjoy ourselves, he's fighting for his life. That is all he knows – from the day he is born, the salmon has to fight to exist. There's always somebody chasing him.

In some ways, the Borders have held on to their rural traditions surprisingly well: it is still the land of the sheep-walk and the salmon-run (though there are also factories producing superconductors and computer parts). The Borders towns and villages are full of people who work nearby, and whose families have been there for many generations. The family seats are occupied still by the Douglases and Scotts, Traquairs and Haigs. But there is at least one prominent new arrival on the scene – forestry.

When Ronnie Rose arrived in the Borders from Loch Lomondside in 1970, most of the hills were still bare, much as they had been for half a millennium. Ronnie comes from a distinguished line of foresters: his grandfather planted trees for Queen Victoria, and his father for her son and grandson, Edward VII and George V respectively. These well-tended forests on the royal estates were quite different to what has since become the norm. They catered for field sports and farming interests as well as timber and, being royal, profit was presumably not the overriding goal. Ronnie Rose is critical of the new forests that have grown up on hill land after the war. He believes that, when investing in new forests, successive governments were tempted into taking economic short-cuts, seduced by the promise of hi-tech methods. He believes that the post-war forestry lobby made the mistake of ignoring nature. Every yard not planted with Sitka or some other fast-growing spruce was regarded as a yard wasted, as profit lost. Nor was there much thought about the effect such dense plantings would have on the landscape and on the environment. As a result they managed to acidify the water supply, ruin the natural drainage and hem in the formerly open scenery. They also forgot that when wet soil freezes it turns Sitka spruce into Bonsai trees. It all helped to give forestry a bad name.

In his own area of responsibility, Ronnie Rose tried to avoid the worst excesses of post-war forestry. 'I have to plan this forest to ensure that the timber goes to the saw mill at year 45. I'll only do that by working with nature, not against it.' He sets the trees well back from the streams, and has put in sump drains to avoid the kind

of flash-flooding that threatened to wash away the salmon nurseries in the headwaters of the valley. And Ronnie's team do their best to be good neighbours, helping to cull the deer and foxes that shelter beneath the dark boughs.

The Duke of Buccleuch believes that the forests are much better designed today than in the past, and dismisses the 'antis' as 'immensely conservative'. He excuses the unattractive, single-aged blocks of trees as something of a rush job, a desire to replace as quickly as possible the woods chopped down by Canadian lumberjacks during the war. 'We've now reached the stage where most of those trees are being cut down. We produce something like 49 000 tons [50 000 tonnes] of timber on the Buccleuch estates every year, and we're able to replant these woods in a much more attractive way, using a mixture of species, including native hardwoods, and creating a structure of different ages.'

Andrew Hepburne-Scott, on the other hand, believes that the forestry lobby has sacrificed the beauty of the Borders for economic gain. He is not against the forests as such, but is critical of their monotony and their all-engulfing size.

What is lacking in the hills is the old, traditional woodland of oak, ash and birch, with their lovely seasonal colours, whereas these spruces are the same uniform green all year round. The regional planners seem to judge everything from the point of view of the motorized traveller. We're told that if a forest is planted out of sight of the road it doesn't matter because it won't be seen. But when you walk over the hills, you find this great barrier. We're increasingly being hemmed in, here in the Borders. My grandfather always used to stop his car near the border so that he could look down from the Cheviot Hills on to the 'promised land' beyond. Today, though, you find this great wall of conifers on the skyline as you drive up from the English side. I feel that is not how I'd like to be welcomed to Scotland.

A second change is rural depopulation, the replacement of farm labourers by machine-run fields and woods that have turned into cellulose crops. The estates are forced to lay off staff to remain financially viable. In the past, estates like The Hirsel could afford to keep on men who did nothing but keep the place tidy,

The fate of much of the Borders landscape:
'We're being hemmed in … the same uniform green
all year round.'

trimming hedges and branches, maintaining paths and so on. In the years preceding the First World War the estate had thirteen men working in the 2-acre (0.8-hectare) walled garden alone, as well as a house full of butlers, cooks and maids. Today the Douglas-Homes run the place themselves with the help of two part-timers. As in other parts of Britain, mechanization has made the unskilled farm labourer virtually redundant. Caroline remembers as the worst day of her life the time when the family was forced to reduce the estate staff. 'It was a terrible thing to have to tell them, but we made it as painless as we could and worked out a redundancy scheme. Nobody was put out of their houses or anything like that, but we were pilloried in the press for it all the same.'

This emptying of the countryside, the replacement of men and women with tractors and trees, strikes at the heart of Borders life, for in such an area nearly everyone who lived in the country worked on one of the estates. Boatman's daughter Rena Walk regrets the passing of the bonds of loyalty that were forged on the estate, the sense of privilege and the shared life. Something of the same confidence in the future has also gone. 'When you came of working age, the girls usually became seamstresses or entered domestic service as housemaids or kitchen maids. The boys went on to the estate, into the forestry, or gardening or the stables. The whole family was employed on the estate, you see. That's all finished now, and with it the community life and the loyalty.'

As Elizabeth Taylor sees it, 'Some people don't want outsiders to come to live in the Borders. We want to keep it to ourselves, the quiet roads, the low level of trouble and crime. But our children can't find work. I've got four children and none of them could have worked here, so you lose your children if you decide to stay. It's a great place to bring up children, but not a place to keep them unless you have a family business that can accommodate them. There's a danger of the Borders becoming the place for the old, and the very young.'

All the same, there remains an inner vitality in the Borders that has sustained the region in good times and bad. As the horses of the Common Ridings pound and splash their way across the river, and the bars of fishing hotels fill up, and the Scott pilgrims gather at Abbotsford, it is hard to imagine the Borders ever losing their unique flavour. The river will always wind down from the hills to the sea, a silver thread linking landscapes and memories. For, as Tennyson reminded us, 'Men may come, and men may go, But I go on for ever.'

SOME TRADITIONAL
BORDERS SALMON RECIPES

The Jake Harvey no-nonsense method

My favourite way of cooking a salmon is to bring the water almost to the boil,
put in a little salt, and then pop in the fish. Take the pan or the kettle off the boil
and allow the fish to cook as the water cools. That way you don't overcook the
salmon, and the flesh remains firm and slightly rare. When the water is cold,
remove the fish, add a little hollandaise sauce and off you go.

The Rena Walk variant

My own way is this. You put the salmon in your fish kettle, and add a very
little water, a couple of carrots and seasoning. Put the lid on and steam for
3 minutes exactly. If you overdo it you take the colour out of it. The flesh
should be lovely and pink. Remove the top skin, put an olive in its eye-socket
and slices of lemon down the side, and that's it, all ready for the table.

The Jim Walker old traditional

The traditional way of cooking salmon at Berwick is to put as much salt as you
can into the water and bring it up to the boil. The salmon is left in the hot water
to cook for a few minutes, and that's it. The traditionalists like it very salty.
The word is 'wersh' – pulls your lips together.

The Elizabeth Taylor improvement

I used to use a fish kettle, but it is too big for my oven now. The ideal way to
cook salmon is with an Aga stove. Just pop it into the kettle with a little water
and white wine, lemon and herbs, and simmer for a short time. Delicious.

David Hodgkiss's Norwegian hearsay

What you do in Norway, I understand, is to dig a hole in the ground, drop in
your fillets of salmon, and build up a layer of more salmon alternating with dill.
Then you add some weights to compress it and go away for six months or a
year, or something like that. When you come back, the salmon should be ready
to eat, something like smoked salmon without the smoke.

— Chapter Seven —

Reeds in the Wind

THE NORFOLK BROADS

WHILE SOME WILD LANDSCAPES are perhaps an acquired taste, the appeal of the Broads seems universal. If a modern Capability Brown was asked to design an outdoor adventure playground in the heart of the countryside, he might well come up with something very close to the Broads: a mingling of land and water, of reed-thatched cottages and brick windmills, of weed-winding channels opening into spacious waters reflecting the sails and the cumulus clouds of the huge East Anglian sky. Above all, he would realize the truth of an epigram of the landscape writer Nan Fairbrother: that few of us really want 'to get away from it all'. What we prefer, when all is said and done, is 'to get half away from some of it'. In the difference between the two you have the old Broads and the new. Before the war this was a quiet area, certainly popular for boating, but for boats with sails, not engines. You arrived by rail and, unless you were lucky enough to be a member of a shooting party on one of the private estates, you made your own entertainments. It is different today. The Broads can still appear wild and beautiful, but they have to cater for family holidays and weekenders on pleasure boats, in restaurants and

Horsey Mill, an eighteenth-century windmill which
helped drain the marshes in the area.

shopping centres, on conducted tours. The Broads have become, in fact, a National Park – a people's playground – in all but name. And to an even greater extent than other English and Welsh National Parks, the Broads have to face the apparently irreconcilable claims of mass tourism and wilderness.

The Broads have long been an important waterway. Before the railways and surfaced roads, most of the freight between Yarmouth and Norwich – coal, grain, merchandise – went by water, carried in the hold of those lovely, dark-sailed, shallow-drafted wherry boats beloved by landscape artists. And to experience the Broads fully you still need a boat. Preferably a sail boat, so you can hear the birds and smell the waterside plants as you move slowly downriver. David Dane, one of the latest of a long line of distinguished Norfolk artists, actually used a boat as his studio because he felt that the only way to capture the special Broads atmosphere in paint was to experience it as he reached for his brushes.

> The most vivid memories I have are of the Broads in the early morning, waking up on a boat somewhere in the marshes, the dark sails of the wherries already lumbering through the reedbeds, watching the mist rise off the water, the wakening of birdlife, the elegant reeds – to me, the most beautiful plants in the world, reflecting the seasons so perfectly. I still put wherries in my paintings, even though they have become a rare sight. Somehow the modern power-cruiser doesn't seem part of the scene.
>
> I don't think it is a coincidence that Norfolk has produced so many land-scape artists, from Crome and Cotman onwards. It's to do with the quality of the light here – the breathtaking sunsets in autumn with the reeds turning gold and the geese flying out over the marshes. In my pictures I try to capture the essence of the Broads, the true feeling of a particular area and not just a pretty scene. They are partly based on my childhood experiences here, on my first visionary memories, and painting these scenes is rather like experiencing my childhood again. I've been fortunate in having developed a certain recognizable style – a particular, personal way of seeing things.

Growing up in this reedy wilderness could mark a person for life: experiencing the sense of adventure and the intimate contact with nature, like a storybook unfolding, as you explored the dykes and waterways in your small boat. David Dane felt this strongly:

Cargo wherries with their dark sails were one
of the familiar sights of the Broads up until the
late 1930s.

My family moved to the Broads in the late 1940s, after my widowed mother
married a Norfolk reed-thatcher. It was then a very wild district, and so far as I
was concerned, nobody had ever explored it before. It was my wilderness and I
was its discoverer. I remember the journeys by row boat or raft, through waters
sometimes choked with lilies, with the strange calls of marsh birds in the reeds,
the foghorn booming of the bittern. Around the bend of the river there might be
a little reed-thatched cottage with smoke curling from its chimney, and I used to
wonder who lived there and what they did. There were so many fish – eels, roach,
rudd and bream – I used to pull them out by the score and bring them home to
feed the cats.

For Keith McDougall, too, many memories are to do with the sights, sounds and scents of nature, experienced with young eyes full of wonder.

> I grew up on a Broads estate after my father bought Catfield Hall, situated half-way between Hickling and Barton Broads. I used to come home to Wroxham station at the start of the school holidays, and remember being met by this incredible heady scent, the scent of the Norfolk fens and the river. You heard the ducks calling overhead, and the pheasants going up to roost in the alder carr. I couldn't wait to get into the punt and off into the dykes next day. Even lying in bed there were the night sounds. Barn owls nested in the hollow elm tree yards from my window, and on a few nights every spring there would be an incredible noise when all the frogs and toads for miles around seemed to be mating in our dyke.

Small wonder, then, that so many Broadlanders are expert naturalists. This is one of the Meccas of natural history, the best opportunity to see rare and wonderful breeding birds like marsh harriers, bitterns and bearded tits, unfamiliar passage birds in the spring and autumn, and an incredible variety of beautiful wild flowers and insects. Michael Seago remembers the extraordinary bird-watching opportunities during the war, when much of the Broads was a restricted area. It was very different then, almost desolate, but with reminders of wartime activity everywhere. The larger Broads were full of empty oil drums and old hulks and houseboats, to prevent enemy seaplanes landing. Halvergate Marshes were festooned with a lattice of iron girders, with the oblivious cattle grazing in between. For a while, Breydon Water near Yarmouth was crammed with dummy invasion craft as part of the D-Day deception plan. As a resident, and a free-roaming boy, Michael had the place to himself, cycling along deserted droves with binoculars hidden under his coat. One day he saw six glossy ibises and a white-tailed eagle. Today such a sighting would bring in the 'twitchers' from one end of the country to the other, their electronic pagers bleeping urgently, but Michael was a lone witness in the reeds and marshes. The winter brought new sights: the twice daily passage of geese, skein after honking skein. Good 'vole years' accompanied by an invasion of short-eared owls, which roosted in derelict marshmen's cottages. 'As you approached one of these little houses, owls would erupt from broken windows and doorways, and circle overhead angrily, making their marvellous barking calls.'

A bittern, peering cautiously from the safety of the reeds.
It has almost completely disappeared from the Broads.

One of the most potent sounds of the old Broads was the call of the male bittern. It is known as a 'boom', for want of a better word. Some compare the doleful sound with that made by blowing over the mouth of an empty bottle; indeed, 'bottle-bumper' is one of the old country names for a bittern. It reminds Keith McDougall of cattle lowing in the distance. So familiar was the sound that the boats' foghorns sounding off the Yarmouth coast were known as 'sea bitterns'. Keith used to lie in bed listening with the window open: 'I can honestly say I've been kept awake by bitterns. And covered with mosquito bites on their behalf, too.'

While the bittern's boom is not particularly loud, it carries remarkably, and in the right conditions can be heard more than a mile away. And so, although bitterns never numbered above sixty or so booming males even in the 1950s, everyone heard them. The call was more familiar than the bird that made it for, like the nightingale, the bittern sings offstage – from deep cover among the reeds. It was because they were seldom caught in the act that people believed that bitterns boomed by sticking their beaks in the mud and blowing! When naturalist Percy Trett managed to watch the private life of the bittern at close-quarters, the truth turned out to be much more prosaic. 'The bird sits bolt upright, and flicks its head up and down. Then out it comes – "beeoooom!" Just like that.'

It pays to be wary of some birds at very close-quarters. Percy will never forget his first encounter with a wounded bittern.

> I was about thirteen at the time, unaware of the habits of bitterns and herons, and not as cautious as I should have been. The bittern will crouch with its head curled back until you come near, like I did, and bend over to examine it. That's the moment when they strike, like lightning, straight at your eyes. Luckily for me, the bittern missed my eye but one mandible of its sharp beak went up a nostril while the other clamped shut on the outside. Then the wretched bird pulled with all its might, cutting my nose quite badly. I nearly shook hands with his windpipe, I can tell you!

Today the bittern has become a casualty of the changing waterscape of the Broads. Only two booming males were heard in 1994, and the 'bottle-bump' is no longer a familiar Norfolk sound: the boom has gone bust. The reasons for this dramatic decline are still a matter of debate. They are certainly not the same as those that caused the temporary extinction of the British bittern in the nineteenth century – shooting and egg-collecting. Keith McDougall blames the fox, which was almost unknown in the Broads before the 1950s. Michael Seago, who has monitored breeding bitterns every year since 1954, points to the drying-out of the reedbeds and the decrease in the kind of medium-sized fish the bittern likes, such as small eels. But perhaps the decline is not so very mysterious after all. Almost every change over the past forty years has been to the bittern's disadvantage: more disturbance, more wash from motorcraft, dirty water, dead fish and thick scrub where the reed-cutter used to swing his scythe. Today, conservationists are trying to improve conditions in Broadland nature reserves, cutting the scrub and excavating ponds. Perhaps, in time, the Broads will boom again.

Broadland birdlife also attracted sportsmen. Hickling estate was managed as a private duck shoot, in the charge of the renowned gamekeeper-naturalist Jim Vincent. Jim loved watching wild birds and his rule was benign – he tolerated a few pairs of marsh and Montagu's harriers, and his expertise in nest-finding helped one naturalist to secure the first-ever pictures of a nesting bittern and its brood (the series of pictures was published over two editions of *Country Life,* and paid for the camera). One of Jim Vincent's responsibilities was the organization of the annual coot-shoot on Hickling Broad, a unique event in the sporting calendar. In midwinter, the resident coots were joined by others from Holland and the Rhine and, on occasion, as far away as Poland; thousands of birds arrive, attracted by a large, secluded lake near the coast, comparatively free of boat traffic and full of delicious waterweeds (there was one particular weed, the holly-leafed naiad, that only grew at Hickling and, one must assume, provided a rare delicacy for the more discerning coot).

It was an honour to be invited to the coot-shoot. Keith McDougall's father was a regular on the gun line, and Keith still remembers his sense of excitement and anticipation as he laid out his equipment – shotgun, waterproof cartridges, water-proof coat, hat – on the eve of the great event. The shooting party would assemble at Whiteslea Lodge (perhaps ironically, now owned by the Norfolk Wildlife Trust), where a flotilla of punts was moored ready, one gun per boat, each with a polesman in the stern. The procession would set off down the dyke, fanning out as it reached the open broad. The keeper, armed with a megaphone, would maintain the guns in line as they swept westwards across the lake in crescent formation, driving the coots before them. Guest on the coot-shoot, Michael Boardman, recalls what happened next.

> Now the coot doesn't like to leave the broad. When cornered, its instinct is to fly back over the guns. This provided a more sporting shot than it might sound, because you weren't allowed to stand up in the boat and so had to shoot from a sitting position, which made it very difficult to swing your gun. Ideally there would be a fair headwind, which made the coot fly upwards. A low-flying bird might be an easier shot, but it was felt that there was little sport in shooting a bird that had no chance. On a good day the shoot might bag up to a thousand birds. It made no difference to the numbers, though – next winter, the broad would be just as full of coots.

The dead birds were picked up by other boats as the guns retreated back across the broad, driving the remaining coots across the butts concealed in the shallows. The

bag was distributed among the villagers. Surprisingly, the coot, being a vegetarian and not a fish-eater, tastes rather good, whether roasted, stewed, baked in pies or made into soup. The locals rated it even above wild duck, and Hickling village is said to have smelt of coot soup for days after a shoot.

On at least one occasion, the risk to the guns was almost as great as to the coots. In 1953, the sea broke through the sea wall while the shoot was in progress. And, on this day of all days, Prince Philip was among the guests, together with the cream of Norfolk society; all rocking in mid-water in their cockle boats as the tide surged up the river. The keeper in charge was thereupon placed in a rare dilemma, for he knew that his daughter was on the coast that day. Where lay his duty – in the rescue of the reigning consort or with his own kith and kin? He chose his daughter,

LEFT The coot-shoot sets out, Hickling 1935.
ABOVE A happy party of guns celebrates a successful day at
Hickling Broad. Jim Vincent, head keeper, is standing first left.

perhaps wisely, for although the shooting party managed to return safely to port, several people caught out on the nearby coast that day were drowned.

Wild and empty of human endeavour as the wilderness of reeds can sometimes seem, the Broads have long provided a living for marshmen and reed-thatchers, working the reedbeds and maintaining the dykes and drains. The Broads themselves are flooded ancient peat cuttings, and so are not natural in the strict sense, as was once believed. And those great, sighing stretches of reed were tended as carefully as any field of grass. At one time, reed-cutting was a viable job, with great appeal to the more independent spirits of East Norfolk. In summer, some reed-cutters used to work on the herring fleets, a job that rewarded them with full-length leather proofs which were waterproof boots, ideal for use in the

183

marshes. It was a way of life, in close proximity with nature, that has almost gone now, although a few, like Eric Edwards, still work the reedbeds each year:

> Reed-cutting is a winter job. You normally start in mid-December and stop at around Eastertime. You can't cut reed until the old leaf has fallen away, and that needs a good frost and a bit of wind. We always cut ours 'double wale', which means we do it on a two-year cycle. We never cut the same reed annually – the 'single wale' – but do one half one year, and the other half the next. The main reason is to minimize disturbance to the wildlife, so there is always plenty of growing reed to hide in. Reed-cutters use machinery most of the time nowadays, but I still have a lot of affection for the old scythe. It comes back into its own when there's a lot of standing water in the marshes. The strongest reeds usually grow in water, especially where the tide floods in regularly.
>
> You shouldn't cut reed when it's wet – if you tie it wet, it won't dry out properly and might rot when the thatcher stores it. So I wait for the sun, until all my reeds are nice and dry. I like to cut very low, because I was taught that the best bit of the reed is at the bottom, and it also keeps the marsh nice and clean. You have to rake out all the debris, by hand normally. The old boy taught me how to keep the bundles of reeds nice and smart, removing all the old grass and rubbish. We load them on to the punt, which takes about fifty bundles. That's why all these little channels through the reeds are maintained and cleared out regularly: to transport the reed out of the marsh and on to the staithe where the thatcher picks it up. It's used mainly for thatching. They say Norfolk reed lasts a lifetime, and there's still plenty of demand for it from all over the country, so long as it's cut and cleaned right.

Although this is work for the hardy, it is warmer than you might imagine in the middle of the reedbed, sheltered from the wind and with the winter sun slanting down.

> It's privileged work in some ways, but it's hard work, too. You get used to the bitter wind, the frost, ice and snow, but it takes time. I actually enjoy it. You take the rough with the smooth, the calm sunny days as well as the cold rain. But I miss the old boys, the real craftsmen who drew the dykes by hand and cut the reeds the old way. I think the scythe is on the way out now. And it's difficult to

attract young people into this kind of work. I trained two young lads in the reed-cutter's arts, but both have moved on to other things. It's a different world now.

Wesley Tooley became a marshman in the 1930s, learning the skills from his grandfather, the head man of a 1000-acre (404-hectare) level on Halvergate Marshes. In those days, the pastures of Halvergate were famous for their grazing quality. Wesley used to look after store cattle sent all the way from Ireland, by boat, rail and, finally, drove road, for fattening on the marshes. No artificial fertilizers or top dressings were used. The grass was fed only by silt and by cow muck, and in early summer it became a yellow mass of buttercups. The big Norfolk skies always seem especially huge at Halvergate; sometimes the summer clouds seem to press down on you – an enormous weight of air and vapour, under which the walker can feel small and rather vulnerable. Marshmen like Wesley were employed by farmers to keep an eye on the cattle and feed them on marsh hay in the autumn, when the goodness had gone out of the grass. They were paid by the number of cattle they looked after, and by the length of the dykes and drains that they cleared. Most of their work was done using hand tools, and of these there was a bewildering range: hodders and heaving tools for digging, wooden shovels for scooping out the mud from the dykes, hay-rakes or cromes, and a netted iron frame called a dydle for removing floating weed. The marshmen generally lived locally, in thatched cottages within easy reach of the fields. There were no Land Rovers or mobile phones; the men knew the marshes intimately because they experienced them on foot, twelve hours a day, summer and winter, fair weather and foul.

Halvergate Marshes lie close to sea level, and farming them relies on pumped drainage. This was the purpose of those evocative landmarks of the marshes, the windmills. Strictly speaking they are not mills at all but wind *pumps*. Their purpose was not to grind corn but to turn the great paddle-wheels which drew out the springwater and rainwater through the network of drains and into the rivers. The slatted wooden sails would turn on the gentlest of breezes. Michael Seago has a vivid memory of 'the cascades of foaming water' that surged down the main drains on windy days. But when the sails stopped turning, during heavy rain or on the rare calm days, the levels simply flooded. This, of course, suited the wildlife, the marsh flowers and the many birds feeding on the levels, and it was this unpredictable quality that prevented the marshes from supporting any crop more ambitious than wild grass. It was the relative inefficiency of the windmills that

puddled the grass and attracted waders like snipe and redshank to nest among the tussocks in the spring, and thousands of white-fronted and pink-footed geese to feed there in the autumn.

The writing was on the wall for the windmills when a big electric pump station opened at Breydon Water in 1948, capable of drawing 50 tons (51 tonnes) of water per minute. And at a time when the marshman and farm labourer were already a declining species, the mills had become too labour-intensive to maintain: a working windmill needed a man on duty, not least to attend to the little fly-fan at the back which was always jamming. One by one the windmills fell into disuse. Some have since been lovingly restored, but David Dane preferred their former, semi-derelict state: 'Silhouetted against the sky, they were gaunt, like skeletons, with broken spars and their sails falling to pieces.' There is something about Halvergate Marshes that is actually enhanced by ruined buildings and fallen gates – a desolate, ghostly, atmospheric place.

ABOVE Eric Edwards bundling freshly cut reeds.
LEFT Bundles of Norfolk reeds at How Hill.

The more recent history of Halvergate, the public controversy that resulted when some farmers began to drain and then to plough the marshland, is widely known. Halvergate became a byword for the widely felt concern over the future of 'wilderness and wet' in the 1980s. The debate brought protesters and ministers to the marshes, and its echoes reached 10 Downing Street. Eventually the tide turned – an incoming, wet tide. A large part of the marshes is now protected as nature reserves or as Sites of Special Scientific Interest. Ironically, though, it is the geese that have had the last laugh. Although the water levels have been manipulated and raised for their benefit, and at considerable expense, the geese have decided that they now prefer arable crops to marsh grass. 'Thank you for your trouble,' they seem to say, 'but you human beings are not the only animals that can move with the times. I must say, these sugarbeet tops are absolutely delicious!'

On the other hand, one large furry animal that for half a century made itself very much at home in the Broads is there no longer. Coypu were farmed for their valuable fur between the wars and when animals inevitably escaped, or were released, they found the dykes, reedbeds and arable fields of the Broads very much to their liking. In many ways, the Broads resembled their swampy South American homeland, there being plenty of soft shoots to eat, and banks for burrowing into – and no predators either, the only jaguars in Norfolk being the barley barons' motor cars. To begin with, few people worried about the coypus' ability to breed like rabbits, for it was expected that the first hard winter would be the end of them. In any case, the beasts were not without their positive side. Their considerable appetites kept many a dyke free of weeds, and some local people, like the well-known Norfolk naturalist Ted Ellis, were not averse to the occasional coypu steak (Ted also owned a handsome coypu fur hat). At least one smart London restaurant had coypu on the menu, masquerading as 'Argentinian hare'. Ted's widow, Phyllis, remembers the mournful cry of the coypu at night. 'It sometimes sounded like the wail of lost souls out among the swamp and the mist. Or, "horr horr", like a cow coughing. You'd hear them at night, and smell them in the moring – a sour smell.'

Despite appearances, the coypu was harmless to people although, as coypu-trapper Jack Brighton recalls, it could, in certain circumstances, square off with a dog on more than equal terms.

> The coypu was quite a gentle animal and was shy of people. If it saw you first, it would slope off into the reeds or dive into the dyke, where it would swim under-water for maybe 20 yards [18 metres], and come up with just its head showing. If you were still coming, it would dive again, and swim away from you, and if it reached its burrow that would be the last you'd see of it. But it was a different matter with dogs. A dog would attack a coypu on land, but in the water it met its match. A coypu could dive under the dog and come up and bite him, and if it got hold of the dog's ear, it would jerk its head and rip it to ribbons.

The coypu's size and weight were prone to wild exaggeration. Percy Trett:

> I'd heard the old marshmen talking about these 'great old 35-pounders [16 kilo-grams], boy'. I had my doubts, because the largest coypu I'd ever shot was only

Jack Brighton BEM, king of the coypu hunters.

A marsh harrier carrying nest material.
Once among the rarest of birds, it has made
a welcome recovery in recent years.

19 pounds [8.6 kilograms]. So I decided to offer a reward for any coypu over 22 pounds [10 kilograms] – £6 it was, which was a fortune to me in those days. Sure enough, I soon got a call from the pub landlord saying one of the old marsh-men had brought in a dead coypu weighing 22 pounds. 'Hold him there,' I said, 'and I'll come over and give him his six quid.' We went into the back room of the pub and put the coypu on the scales and, right enough, the weight was exactly 22 pounds. I was about to give the old blighter his money, but first I picked the coypu up by the tail. 'You've got a very good coypu here,' I says, shaking it, and suddenly out of its mouth plops this big stone. They'd take your leg off as soon as look at you, the marshmen round here. They're great ones for practical jokes. So he didn't get his money, but I did stand him a beer instead.

Although in hard weather they were reduced to eating one another's tails, the coypu survived. By the 1960s, there were an estimated 200 000 in East Anglia, and the animals had by then become a serious nuisance to the growing number of farmers. Jack Brighton describes the situation:

> You imagine a farmer drilling a field of beet on land reclaimed from the marsh. If there were coypu nearby, they'd get about four leaves through and then you'd find you'd lost a quarter of an acre [0.1 hectares]. They would graze off wheat and barley, and they were forever eating out carrots. Overnight, a colony of coypu could take two or three rows of carrots along the full length of the field. There was also the problem of their burrowing along the sides of the marsh roadway, so you'd get a farm tractor breaking through the surface and dropping down to its axles. Or, in the same way, a cow might take a tumble and break its leg.

The Ministry of Agriculture's answer was an all-out campaign to oust the coypu. Jack Brighton had been trapping coypu in Norfolk for most of his life and, seeing a job for coypu trappers advertised, he thought:

> That's right up my street. It won't be work for me, it'll be as though I'm on holiday, just wandering about looking for coypu. I applied and got the job, but I was in for a bit of a shock. The following Saturday, a little Morris pick-up arrived at my door with sixty traps in the back. I was told to take them to Burgh St Peter, where I met the foreman. He pointed across the marshes to a punt house on the horizon, and said, 'See that? That's the river wall.' And I said, 'Cor, that's a long way.' 'Two miles [3 kilometres], easy. I want you to lay them sixty traps between here and that punt house and then work back to the church at Burgh St Peter. You'll easily dispose of all the traps on that stretch.' Well, this was February, and it was useless trying to take the pick-up into the fields, it'd be up to its axles in mud in no time. 'Christ,' I thought, 'this is going to be a struggle.' And it was, too, manhandling the traps on to the dyke, three under each arm. When a farmer came past on his tractor with a trailer full of hay, I asked him if I could chuck the traps on top. 'Oh, I haven't got time to mess about waiting for you,' he says. 'You'll have to cart them out yourself, the same as the other buggers did.' That was my introduction to coypu-trapping. And all the time, the farmers are watching you like hawks, maybe wondering whether you've taken an extra half-hour on your lunch break. Farmers are all like that, though, aren't they?

It was obviously going to be a long haul. Eventually the campaign was costing £350 000 a year and employing twenty-three trappers and three foremen, including Jack Brighton, whose personal contribution resulted in his award of the British Empire Medal in 1978. Working in pairs, the trappers might catch up to fifty coypu on a good night; on other occasions they caught few or none, or accidentally trapped mink or duck, once even a bittern. In one place, their traps were opened every morning by two well-meaning old ladies, out walking their dogs: 'Well, we felt so sorry for the poor beast inside.' Trapping the coypu became a way of life for the valiant twenty-six – yet another craft in the reedbed world. As coypu-trapper Cyril Clarke recalls:

> It was a great life if you like solitude. Trapping day in, day out, through the winter as well, you felt in tune with nature, in a complete world of your own. You could either reject it completely, or allow it all to sink into your consciousness. You'd witness things you'd normally see only on television – like close-up views of marsh harriers and herons. And meet and chat to the other people sharing the reed world – keepers, reed-cutters, fishermen. In winter, you might go days without seeing a soul. For me, the biggest difficulty was coming back into civilization.

Catching the last few animals was a tedious business, but every single one had to be rounded up. Bitter experience had shown that a few coypus can very quickly turn into a great many. Someone told Jack Brighton that if the coypu was ever eradicated, he would eat his hat. In 1989, Jack sent him the salt and pepper. Personally he has mixed feelings about the success of the campaign: not only about the demise of this gentle, if troublesome, animal, but also about the demise of their own jobs – for in this case ultimate success also spelt redundancy.

But there are other exotic beasts still lurking in the Broads. Sometime after the coypus escaped from their fur-farms, they were joined by muntjac and Chinese water-deer from Woburn Abbey and other ornamental parks. Lurking in some of the Broads are catfish, from no-one-knows-where, some of which are reputed to be giants and 'capable of swallowing a small dog'. According to Percy Trett, the latest outlaws to hide out here are freshwater turtles.

> A few years ago there was the craze for the Mutant Ninja Turtles, and for a short while freshwater turtles became popular children's pets. Well, I don't know

if you've ever kept turtles, but they can soon start to smell to high heaven, and the parents were only too happy to get rid of them. But rather than upset the children by killing them, they released them into the Broads. On Ormesby Broad we've got the red-necked turtle, but unfortunately we've also got the snapper turtle, which can grow quite big. And then they will be quite capable of giving a nasty bite to anyone trailing their foot in the water from a boat.

The rise and fall of the coypu is far from the only change that the Broads have seen since the war. The old clinker-built trading wherries, with their great, dark sails, still glide through the reeds in memory and in paintings, but most were decommissioned long ago. The only one left is *Albion*, which has been restored for boat rides (another, *Maud*, is currently being restored). All other wherries under sail in the Broads were built as pleasure craft or 'wherry yachts' and were never used as cargo boats. The big, powered cruisers of today have enabled thousands of people to enjoy a day out on the Broads and to experience this wonderful waterscape in relaxation and comfort. There has been a price to pay, however. The wash of power boats has damaged reedbeds and banks throughout the Broads, and their very presence detracts from the wilderness that others are seeking. If Phyllis Ellis could change just one thing, it would be to replace the diesel engines with slower electric motors.

> Today we are generally in too much of a hurry. No one has the time to look and savour things in their haste to get from A to B. You can't really experience the Broads in a day. We used to spend two or three weeks on the water, and take it very gently; we'd land and look at churches and around the villages, wander up this river and that, wherever the fancy took us.
>
> You often can't see much from the big pleasure boats, apart from the tops of the reeds. Nor can you listen to the sounds of nature with the engine going and someone playing a transistor radio; nor smell the river and the mint and the bankside flowers through the diesel fumes. What you're missing is the essence of the Broads.

When Ted and Phyllis Ellis moved to their secluded cottage at Wheatfen Broad in 1946, the water was so clear you could see the cast shells and firm sand at the bottom, and the shoals of silvery fish scattering at the prow of the boat. Clean

A boatload of happiness – Phyllis Ellis (second from right)
enjoying an outing to Wheatfen Pool in 1952.

water was the basis of the whole Broadland ecosystem: there were underwater gardens of pondweeds and stoneworts; floating lilies carpeted the shallow broads; and, along the dykes, dragonflies and swallowtail butterflies danced in the scented margins. If you heard splashings and mewing cries, you knew you were sharing the waterscape with otters.

The first sign that things were going wrong was one that many people in fact welcomed – the sudden decline of the notorious Broadland gnats and mosquitoes. The cause appears to have been diesel-powered boats, introduced in the early 1950s. As Percy Trett explains:

> If you spill petrol on to water, it will soon evaporate. But diesel oil doesn't do that. It spreads across the surface, and it lasts. Now the millions of gnat and midge larvae living in the water have to come up to the surface to breathe. They push their tails through the surface, and take in a little air through a kind of snorkel, and then get back to their business again. But when there's a film of oil,

The swallowtail, our largest butterfly, and one
confined to the Broads where it flies around the margins of
reedbeds in late May and June.

they literally can't breathe, and so they die. And this strikes right at the base of
the food chain – fewer gnats biting, maybe, but also less food for swallows, young
fish and other life.

Another pollutant was tepol, a product of the petroleum industry, used in liquid
detergents and washing-up powders. Tepol is rich in phosphates. As Percy puts it,
'the old country girl washes her linen, and does her washing-up, and the effluent
runs down into the dykes, and thence into the rivers. So suddenly you've got

phosphate-rich water.' Gradually, waters that were once gin-clear became turbid, and you could no longer see the shells and pondweeds on the bottom. Soon there were none to be seen. Free-flowing mud came up on the tide, a smothering slick that stuck fast on the ebb tide and plastered itself to the bottom. The outgoing water may have looked clear – but that is because it had dumped its mud in the Broads. Underwater plants died and decayed into mud themselves.

But the most serious threat to the old Broads came not from within but from the surrounding land. The water had owed its clarity to the low productivity of the surrounding farmland; in other words, rural poverty and clean water went hand in hand. But soon the farmer was able to improve his land, and his income, by fertilizers made not by a cow but by ICI. And for every sack of nitrates that went into the soil, another sackful was washed away by the rain and into the streams and rivers. The Broadland rivers became a kind of waste-pipe for East Anglia's farming boom. At the same time, the motor car brought unprecedented numbers of people to the Broads, and some of them, understandably, fell in love with the area, and moved there on retirement. Ever since man became a settler he has been a phosphate producer, from domestic and garden rubbish, and sewage. Much of that went into the Broads, too. As Keith McDougall observes sadly, 'I don't think anyone swims in Barton Broad any more.'

The increase of sediment dumping, from nature's $\frac{1}{25}$ inch (1 millimetre) a year to the $\frac{4}{5}$ inch (2 centimetres) of recent years, means that, in theory, the Broads will no longer exist in fifty years' time. They will fill up with mud and dry out. This theoretical Doomsday is being countered by dredging machines that suck up the mud like giant vacuum cleaners, and by sewage-treatment works that 'strip' the water of phosphates before it enters the Broads. But there is no doubt that much of the Broads is drier than it was. Phyllis Ellis remembers squelching across the open fen to take the children swimming. 'Now, we'd have to take a hatchet with us. No one mows the marshes or cuts the reed now, and it has become overgrown with sallow bushes. In the old days, nobody would have wasted good reed like that. People were poor and needed the money – somebody would have cut it, tied it and sold it.'

It is easy to present the loss of water quality as a tale of doom and gloom. But it would probably have been impossible to raise living standards in the area, and also to cater for mass tourism from the towns and cities, without damaging the environment. It is the price that most residents and visitors have been willing, consciously or not, to pay. The marshmen who led such colourful and apparently contented existences lived in tied cottages with no electricity, no running water and outside loos full of gnats. Few people, retiring from life in an office in the city, on comfortable savings and a pension, would be willing to forgo their comforts for the privilege of living in beautiful, natural surroundings. On the contrary, most modern sailing boats on the Broads have their own gas cookers, shower units, and even television sets.

City money that helped to pollute the Broads can also be used to conserve it. Today, large areas are owned by conservation bodies, and Broadland as a whole is the responsibility of an authority with wide-ranging powers (and a big budget) to reconcile farming, tourism and the environment. Cautious optimism for the future is now possible, not least because no one wishes to damage the Broads and their wildlife any further. But there are some, like Cyril Clarke, who remember the pre-war and immediate post-war years and naturally regret the loss of the old carefree life implied in all the new rules and regulations.

> When I was young, every sailing trip was an adventure. If you felt like staying on the river overnight, you just moored up, and scrounged a few eggs and some milk from a cottage. Now it is about as adventurous as the Number 4 bus. The conservation bodies vie with each other to buy up the Broads, and they've all got their long list of 'must do's' and 'can't do's'. So I find it hard to enjoy the place in quite the same way.

Perhaps, like everywhere else, the beauty of the Broads is in the eye of the beholder. There is still wilderness and peace here for those who want to roam, and although the 'honeypots' certainly swarm with holiday-makers in the summer, it is not difficult to avoid them. Phyllis Ellis has lived here for more than half a century. Her cottage in the reeds is now at the centre of a nature reserve, open 365 days a year, and dedicated to the memory of her late husband, Ted Ellis, 'the people's naturalist'. Although she sometimes thinks it would be nicer if Norfolk was a bit warmer, she would never contemplate moving anywhere else. She must speak for hundreds of people who have lived and worked among the reeds and by these luscious, sail-brimmed waters.

POSTCARD

— Chapter Eight —

In Search of Wilderness

THE SCOTTISH HIGHLANDS

IS THERE ANY REAL WILDERNESS left in Britain? In the remotest parts of the Highlands, perhaps, or somewhere among the mosaic of land and water in the Outer Hebrides, or in some deep secret ravine? To ask the question begs a different question: what is wilderness? Does it mean something utterly wild and untouched, a virgin land ruled solely by nature; or is it more of a concept, suggesting that each one of us may regard wilderness differently, according to our own experiences and inclinations? Perhaps we all have our own specific, personal wilderness, which might even be close to home.

Probably most would agree that the wilderness has a number of desirable qualities. We prefer at least the illusion of wildness, a big, empty, lonely place, expressed by the writer Lionel Griffiths as: 'The feeling of being a stranger in a landscape unmarked by man.' We would rather not be reminded of the dominion of humankind in the form of surfaced roads, lines of pylons or helicopters buzzing overhead. We would hope, like Sir Walter Scott, to find grand scenery: 'Brown heath and shaggy wood, mountain and flood.' And wild animals and plants that

Wilderness – or nearly. The headwaters of the Dee
trickle down from the Lairig Ghru Pass, past the conical
peak of Devil's Point.

seem to embody the wild spirit of the place, like an eagle soaring high in the sky or ancient Caledonian pines rooted in moss and heather. Many people would know wilderness when they find it, in a sudden uplifting of the heart, or a transcendent feeling of peace, even humility, among elemental surroundings. Perhaps, deep down in most of us, there is a blood memory of primitive living, something made all the more desirable by the artificiality of the lives we lead today.

Some people seem to feel this more strongly than others. Syd Scroggie's love of the remote, mountainous places of Scotland lies at the very centre of his life. Wilderness provides him with solace and fulfilment, and inspires his poetry.

Syd Scroggie

People go to the hills for all kinds of reasons. They look for flowers, or check rocks and geologize, study weather or watch birds. Nobody's more interested in these things than me, but I don't walk in the hills for those reasons. They are all on the periphery. The main reason, however you analyse it, is a personal one, to do with feeling. I know when I come to the wilderness that I belong here – among the sounds of the high tops, the ptarmigan croaking amid the boulders on Macdui, the river running below, the liquid pipe of the golden plover, so evocative of the wild open country. Whenever I experience it, I'm still reminded of my first original hill experience, when we biked up from Dundee just before the war and camped out in the Lairig Ghru.

Syd Scroggie's experience of wilderness is different from that of most of us, and perhaps richer, because he is blind.

I trod on a shoe mine at Cassino and got blown up. I remember lying in the hospital in Naples, blind and minus a leg, waiting for the boat to take me back home. One day a pal of mine told me: 'There's a Scots lassie in the neighbouring ward who wants to meet you.' She'd just had her appendix out, and she came in, saw this mountain of bandages and said, 'Is there a Scotsman in there?' 'Aye, it's me.' So we started chatting, and it soon became clear she loved the hills as much as I did. We had a long talk about the Cairngorms and the Lairig Ghru. I didn't see May

McFarlane again for another twenty years, until she called on me at home. She told me that I'd said something in that hospital which she'd always remembered: 'I can do without my eyes, but I can't do without my mountains.'

I did get back to the hills in the end, but it took a long time. And I found out that although I was walking blind with a guide, it didn't make much difference. I discovered that for me the wilderness experience isn't an external one. I don't need to see it. It was something that happened inside, a quasi-religious experience. I felt at one with the surroundings in that kind of environment, in the wild country.

Adam Watson has probably spent more days in the Cairngorms than anyone alive. An upland ecologist, and a world expert on grouse and ptarmigan, he shares Syd Scroggie's passion for the wild. Although he doesn't 'dislike company, depending on who the company is', he feels that wilderness, like star-gazing, is best savoured alone, without the distractions. He first felt the call of the wild on reading Seton Gordon's book, *The Hills of Scotland*, at the age of nine.

As soon as I opened it and started reading and looking at the photographs, that book changed the world for me. It was as though someone had switched a light on. Gordon had this ability to catch the mystery and wonder and beauty of the place, and its wildness. He didn't overwrite; he wasn't a sentimentalist, and didn't talk about dangers or the spirit of the wild, but he was a natural hillman, and I started to see things through his eyes. I didn't then regard the Cairngorms as a wilderness, just as a wonderful place I couldn't get to often enough.

Adam Watson

I've had hundreds of best days in the Cairngorms. Wilderness to me is an area which has been shaped by natural forces – weather, vegetation and animals – not by man. To some extent I think it's also a concept of the human mind, because it includes things like solitude and even danger. It has other meanings, too. You often read about politicians being out in the wilderness, meaning they've been sacked or something like that, but I think most scientists would see it as an area that is relatively natural. The high tops of the Cairngorms are more or less as Mother Nature left them. In fact, arguably, this is the best wilderness area in the EU, outside the Scandinavian countries.

Dick Balharry, too, has spent much of his life working in mountainous country, first as a nature reserve warden at Beinn Eighe in Wester Ross, and later in the Cairngorms. He knows that to search for land completely unstained by man is to quest in vain, that you can find human footprints on virtually every inch of land outside the polar areas. To him, however, ecological purity is not the point. It is how you *experience* wildness that matters more.

> Wilderness to me is somewhere where you can find complete solitude, and feel rejuvenated by close contact with nature. The word has difficulties for me, because you could apply it to parts of the Highlands that are not strictly wilderness: they are deserted, because the people have been pushed out. My wilderness is wild land, where you can walk and feel the past all round you – like the remnants of the ancient pine forests. I call it God-fearin' country, not because I'm religious in the strict sense, but because it is there that I feel a sense of communion with nature. Wilderness doesn't have to mean a permanent absence of people. You can find wilderness qualities in the sea alone in your little sailing boat, which isn't affected by the fact that an ocean liner went past an hour before. I think you can have wilderness *and* people.

Wilderness, then, is to a great degree in the eye of the beholder, whether mountaineer, scientist, naturalist or tourist. Perhaps what matters most is not what it is, but what it provides for those who seek it: solitude, peace, a restorative sense of harmony. As Syd Scroggie says: 'To find yourself, in some inner way, in that environment.' Some will be contented with the merest dabble, a day walking in the hills and back to the hotel for supper. But Syd believes that the essence of wilderness is only found when camping out in the hills, sleeping beneath the stars and waking with the first shafts of sun slanting into the tent. Few of us will stay there for long, though. Those areas of Britain that remain truly wild are the frontiers that have defied all attempts to tame them. They are the coldest, steepest, wettest, most windswept, most defiantly midge-ridden parts of the landscape. The Cairngorms have more in common with Iceland than Cornwall. It can snow there in any month, and there are a few places where the ice never melts. Although we are

PREVIOUS PAGES Glen Affric, the setting of one of Scotland's grandest and best-preserved ancient forests.

drawn to wild and lonely places to experience something grander than ourselves, sooner or later we will pine for civilization and our back gardens. Adam Watson does not believe that civilized Western man can bear the wilderness for long.

> He's got to take his own food in with him. He may take a tent, or live in a bothy for a while, but he's dependent on supplies from outside. That's very different from the Eskimos or the Lapps who, when I travelled in Arctic Canada in the 1950s, were still living in the wilderness and living off it – and living with it, too; they weren't destroying it.

A few, though, live all year round in places where most of us would feel adventurous if we stayed a weekend. Tom Rigg runs perhaps the most isolated youth hostel in Britain, an old shooting lodge by the shore of Loch Ossian in the central Highlands. You reach it only by the West Highland Railway, from its bleak station at Corrour, or along unmade tracks, by foot or by Land Rover. 'We're 10 miles [16 kilometres] from the nearest pub, and twice that to the nearest shop. On 80 square miles [207 square kilometres] of moorland, bog and hill, there are only eight residents. On the other hand, there are about 2500 free-ranging red deer.'

> I first came here nearly a quarter-century ago. I'm not a mountain man by upbringing, but I've always loved walking and climbing in wild country as an escape from work in the factory. After our children had grown up, my wife let me go. It was an amiable parting: she knew I'd yearned to live in the wild for so long. I set off north along the Pennine Way, and eventually finished my journey here, at Loch Ossian. I took on the job of looking after the hostel for a season, and I've been here ever since. I keep the place clean and warm, light the fire in the morning and pump the water, welcome the new guests and say goodbye to those who are departing. And tell them fireside stories about deer and eagles and foxes. The hostel is open half the year and for the other half I work on the estate, helping with the stalking.
>
> When I have free time during the day, I often set out with my binoculars to see what I can find. Or take Omar Khayyám's advice:
>
> > *A loaf of bread beneath the bough*
> > *A book of verse, a flask of wine*
> > *And thou beside me singing in the wilderness.*

That's not a bad way to see the wildlife. If you're prepared to sit still for a couple of hours, the animals and birds just carry on around you. It's amazing what you will see – martens, eagles, foxes, wildcats, or young ospreys catching fish on the loch.

One of my companions is a tame deer, an old stag I call Windswept. He's here most of the time except during the rut, when he's off for a month to defend his corner, always in the same place and with the same hinds. Hopefully he won't get shot. This estate never shoots any stag with more than eight or nine points on his antlers. They believe in leaving the best stags to breed, so Windswept should be all right so long as he doesn't roam too far. He's a great favourite with the children, and will come into the hostel to be hand-fed. He's particularly fond of bananas. He hasn't actually lain down in front of the fire and gone to sleep yet, but otherwise he makes himself pretty much at home here.

Sharing this wilderness with Tom Rigg is Ken Smith, a true man of the wilds, who, like the American writer Henry Thoreau before him, built himself a cabin on the shore of a lake. Apart from the occasional visit to a far-off supermarket, Ken is more or less self-sufficient. The cabin is heated by a solar panel on the roof, and power is provided by a windmill on a nearby hill. He has a wood-burning stove and what must be the only patio on Rannoch Moor. Like Tom Rigg, he is an incomer.

I used to work in the building trade in the Midlands, doing flooring and travelling all round the big cities. Bloody murder. Then I escaped and went to the Yukon for a couple of years, where I learned how to live rough in a harsh environment and build my own dwelling. Later on I went tramping in the Highlands, camping out or living in bothies. Then I found this place. I got the owner's permission to build a cabin here using the nearby fir plantation as a source of timber. I started in autumn, and 40 days and 105 trees later it was New Year's Eve and I'd got it finished. As it happened, the storm that night was so bad, with trees coming down all round, that I was forced out again, rather than risk a log crashing through the roof. This is the main difference between the Highlands and the Yukon: Scotland is warmer, but it's also much windier. In the Yukon the trees stand there like soldiers all winter, as if frozen. You could take a candle outside, most nights, though you had to use an iron bar to smash through the ice.

A herd of 'the branchy crested race' in grand surroundings.

I've got nearly everything I want out here. I cut wood with my power-saw for the stove. I catch pike and trout in the loch. I grow vegetables and soft fruit in the garden, and make my own wine from practically anything that grows. I rarely get lonely. I get a lot of guests and visitors, especially during the stalking, and there are always things to do.

I must be one of the few people in Britain to be bothered by pine martens. They're a bit of a pest at the moment, stealing fat from the bird-table and mice from the traps, and jumping on to the roof at night. They scratch at the tarred surface, for some reason, so that when there's a downpour water starts coming through the roof. I bang on the wall, which usually gets rid of them – until the next night.

Ken Smith's hermitage is one solution to living in the wilderness, a solitary, contemplative way of life that has been followed by a few since Biblical times. In some ways, though, it represents a dead-end: a cabin in the wilds, so many fish caught, so many mice trapped, a regular diary to remind you of the passage of time and physical existence: as Thoreau put it, it is toeing the line between the past and the future, 'to stand on the meeting of two eternities'. Loch Ossian is a lonely place now, and probably always has been. But the Highlands are also full of artificial wildernesses, places which were once thriving communities and echoed to the sounds of men and women at work and children at play. Toby Robinson, who runs an adventure holiday centre in Knoydart, one of the emptiest parts of Scotland, told us that this was once a relatively well-populated area. 'Its barrenness is of our own making. The people were evicted, and the trees cut down. If it's a wilderness, it is the human species that has made it so.'

Duncan Matheson lives in Camus-luinie in Wester Ross, where he was employed as a stalker. When he was a boy, the glen was a lively, working community. Deer-stalking provided summer work for fifteen young men, in addition to the permanent staff of keepers and stalkers, and the annual invasion of domestic servants and maids to look after the laird and his guests. The unmarried maids met local lads at ceilidhs and dances, and often married them and settled in the glen, bringing in fresh blood and contact with the world outside. 'It all made life go round a bit faster.'

> We used to roam around barefoot a lot of the time. The beauty of living here was that you could roam where you liked, and fish in the streams and hill lochs. We took such freedom for granted, as we did the fresh air. People were poor compared with today, but they didn't starve, they had enough to live on. We had fresh, home-grown food most of the time. The only things we bought regularly were tea, sugar and flour. It was a staple diet – brose [porridge] for breakfast, and a lot of bread, scones, eggs and cheese. We did a lot of walking. So did the postman. He walked 4 miles [7 kilometres] to bring the mail to a lonely keeper's cottage, three times a week. That's better service than you'd get there now. In the pre-war days, when the costs of running Highland estates were so much lower, enough people lived and worked in the glen for it to be a more or less self-sufficient community. You had your village shop, a cobbler and a tailor, a blacksmith and so on.

A stalker's children were normally taught by what was called a side-school teacher, who was usually a single young woman and who gave them their first lessons. She would have her own room in the stalker's house, and soon became one of the family. Some of them, at least, took to the life, and Duncan Matheson knows many Highlanders who look back with great affection to the people that taught them the three R's – reading, writing and 'rithmetic – in those far-off glens.

One such was Johan MacInnes, who first came to the glen, aged seventeen, to teach the gamekeeper's children.

I was there for two-and-a-half happy years. I sometimes used to walk down to spend a night with relatives, or got the regular delivery van to give me a lift home. But for most of the time my family was here, where I worked. It was a small but very close community, mostly shepherds and gillies. I was homesick at first, but I soon settled in and got used to the way of life. There was my daily work to attend to, the school hours and helping with household work and the milking. If you didn't know how to do a thing, you soon learned. The outdoor life changed from season to season. There was peat-digging at the end of winter, then lambing. In summer there was a procession of visitors and guests, beginning with the fishing and later, the high point of the year, the stalking season.

Duncan Matheson takes up the story.

Deer are difficult to stalk, and that's putting it mildly. They have an acute sense of smell, and with the wind in the right direction they can detect you from more than a mile away. What's more, they generally have a sentry on duty when they're feeding, usually a hind, who will sit and watch the land all round for intruders. To get within range, you need to use every bit of cover, little hollows and stream banks. There will be times during the stalk when you're on your hands and knees, or even crawling on your belly. So your deer usually has a good chance of getting away. We normally stalk up to about 100 to 150 yards [90 to 140 metres], depending on how good a shot your guest is. The rifles used are much more accurate than they used to be in the days when they'd use dogs for running down the wounded stag. Most kills are quick and clean now.

I remember once shooting two deer, one a few hundred yards above the other, so that I had to spend some minutes dragging one of them downhill to where I'd shot the first one. As I approached it, I thought there's something funny there – the carcass looked bigger than it should. I got my telescope out and had a quick look, and there was a fox, fastening its teeth on the dead deer's throat, trying to suck the blood out of it before I could get down. It was incredible how quickly it had got there, as though the fox had been stalking me while I stalked the deer. He knew he only had a few moments, you know, and there he was trying to get his belly full.

There are many little stories like that … Anyone who has lived close to wilderness will have tales to tell of their encounters with wild animals. Dick Balharry has kept tame deer, hawks and martens, and will tell you riveting tales at the drop of a deer-stalker's hat. Although his first loves are eagles and pine martens, he has a soft spot for another, not always popular symbol of the wild, the raven.

Ever since I was a boy, I've always kept animals. I love to try and find out how they tick. My first job in the Highlands was as an assistant keeper. I remember being shown the tricks of the trade by the head keeper, all the weapons of war – guns, poison, traps. One of my first jobs was to go out and kill a raven that had decided to nest on the estate. A raven in the spring is a lovely sight – they roll in the air and soar and tumble and croak – beautiful birds. So instead of killing it, I climbed down to its nest and stole the young bird and took it home. I named it Rory. Now, ravens are intelligent birds and can be taught to speak better than parrots. Once it could fly, Rory would follow me around, and one day it flapped in through the open window and into the room, just when I was eating my meal with the keeper and his wife. And he promptly whitewashed the floor. They shouted, 'Get that filthy black bugger of a bird out of here,' and I thought, what a marvellous phrase for Rory to learn. Eventually, after a few months of practice, Rory was able to croak a rough version, though he tended to get stuck with his b's – b-b-bird, or whatever. Eventually the day dawned when we were sitting round the table taking tea with the Minister, in his dark clerical garb, and Rory chose that moment to fly up to the window and croak, 'Get that filthy b-b-black bugger out of here.' The Minister took one look, and decided it was Satan himself who was speaking. The keeper swore he'd kill the bird for this, and possibly me as well. So that was the end of my first job in the Highlands. I packed up and left, with Rory, for Glen Lyon.

Dick was never very happy as a gamekeeper – he loved carnivores and hawks too much to enjoy killing them. In the early 1960s he landed the job of his heart's

Top Pine marten – 'the size of a small cat,
with warm-brown fur.'
Above Golden eagle and chick on a remote Scottish hillside.

desire, as the warden of one of the then Nature Conservancy's largest and wildest nature reserves: Beinn Eighe, a vastness of sandstone ridges, natural amphitheatres and ragged woods of birch and ancient pine. At that time the pesticide scare, made world-famous by Rachel Carson in her book *The Silent Spring*, was at its height. Many birds of prey were deserting their nests or laying stillborn eggs, and one of the suspected causes was the poison used in sheep dips. To Dick fell

211

the arduous and sometimes perilous job of examining the nests of wild golden eagles. 'If eagles were ingesting poison from mutton carrion, it occurred to some of us that people eat more mutton than eagles. You could regard them as a kind of miner's canary, warning us of a polluted environment.'

One of his first close encounters with an eagle might easily have been his last.

I'd climbed up a cliff to examine this particular nest. I could see recent nest material there, and I wanted to see if the eagle had laid any eggs. When I was just below the nest, I scanned the sky with my binoculars to see if the parent bird was about. Far away, maybe half a mile up in the blue sky, I spotted it, like a golden orb with the sun reflected on its feathers. As I followed it, the eagle decided to descend. I never realized how quickly they could fall out of the sky. It got bigger and bigger in my binoculars, its wings spread out, the outstretched talons open, and its leg feathers fluffed up by the wind. Down it came, nearer and nearer, until it filled my vision and I remember thinking, my God, she's going to come down right on top of me. You could hear the noise, sshhh, as the wind passed through her feathers. Then her tail fanned out, and her wings opened, and with incredible grace she just floated on to the eyrie, shuffled on to the eggs and settled down like a broody hen. I've never seen the like again – a plummet of maybe 4000 feet [1200 metres] in a matter of seconds.

Beinn Eighe is also the home of pine martens, which were then regarded as our rarest and most elusive wild mammal. Few zoologists had ever seen one alive in its natural Highland setting. Even the person actually studying martens in Scotland had to content himself with their tracks and droppings. Dick Balharry was determined to get to know these almost legendary animals.

I'll never forget the day I saw my first marten at close-quarters. It was typical marten country, with a good cover of pine and birch trees and plenty of undergrowth for their favourite prey, voles. Suddenly it was there, half-way up a tree, this beautiful animal about the size of a small cat, with warm-brown fur and an apricot-coloured throat and lovely gold-trimmed ears and whiskers. It was a female, and I knew it would have young nearby. Sure enough, clambering over the rocks I could hear them mewing and spitting over some food their mother had brought in. I was trying to worm my way to get a look at them when the mother suddenly appeared again and actually pounced on my shirt. In an instant, I felt these very sharp claws on my arm, non-retractable because they are designed for climbing, and then she was gone. It was a warning – she was telling me I shouldn't be here, you know, and to go away. Which is what I did. They are amazing animals, the fastest sprinters we have, and they can actually chase squirrels through the trees and catch them. Where can you find a more magical animal?

I remember once watching an eagle's nest when the great bird came in with a dead marten to feed to its chicks. As you can imagine, I felt pretty torn – here were the two creatures I love most, and here was one of them, still warm and limp, being fed to the other. But that's the nature of life in places like this.

The demands on our dwindling store of wilderness have steadily grown since the 1930s, when pilgrims like Syd Scroggie would arrive on battered push-bikes, dressed in ragged jumpers, cut-down raincoats and ex-army boots and, as often as not, wet through. Syd remembers three kinds of hill walkers before the war: 'The pass-stormers, the bothy-whackers and the Munro-baggers.' The real wilderness men rather looked down on the collecting instincts of the Munro-baggers, who were keen to climb as many as possible of the hills of 3000 feet [914 metres] or more tabulated by Sir Hugh Munro, the geographer. 'They were a fairly rare breed then, but they've multiplied since.' As for the bothies:

They used to be used by deer-stalkers as temporary accommodation, but then the climbers and walkers took them over. They used to be in a dreadful state, with crumbling walls and rain coming through the roof. But, you see, we Scots love to sit and philosophize, we're not so bothered about keeping ourselves comfortable. But when English walkers started coming to the Cairngorms in numbers, they decided this wouldn't do, and started smartening them up with new slates and window panes. They're a practical race, the English. We would never have done it ourselves. Now Corrour Bothy, which I used to use a lot, was a real bothy. The floor had gone, the panelling stripped away by vandals and what furniture there had been had been burnt. There was an old mattress, but according to rumour it was infested with fleas, so we avoided it. But through the doorway you could see the rippling River Dee and hear the call of the sandpipers, and the croak of grouse, and look across to the great scree slopes of Carn-a'Mhaim. I spent wonderful days at that place, climbing the rocks and exploring the hills.

The trouble with the Cairngorms now is that you find yourself all too often sharing your cliff-face or distant glen with fellow seekers after wilderness. Nor does every-one wish to leave the sophistications of life behind them. Subdued clothing has been replaced by coloured anoraks and elaborate tents. Syd has heard mobile tele-phones ringing from rucksacks half-way along the Lairig Ghru, to him an audible scar, a brutal dissonant chord cutting through the natural sounds of the hills. Remote places are steadily being opened up by the all-too-visible scars of bulldozed tracks. 'It is a terrible mistake. Wilderness land should take you back to the beginning of mankind. It shouldn't be easy to reach.'

The northern slopes of Cairngorm are now an arena for downhill skiing, the most sociable of sports, and there have been planning battles fought between those who wish to expand further and others who want to keep the rest of the hills invio-late. Adam Watson remembers the area before development began in the 1960s.

> You got here along a pot-holed dirt road from Glenmore, ending in a rough track to the summit. We came here for the cross-country skiing, because it was one of the best snow-lying areas in Scotland. There are now ski-tows on different parts of the hill, as well as the chairlift and the high-level restaurant. There are a lot of paling fences round the place, which reduce the wind and prevent the snow from blowing away. This is the main difference between Scottish and Alpine skiing. Scottish skiing is on bare, sometimes windswept, slopes, and you need a double line of fences on either side of the tow to provide a ribbon of snow on which the skiers can be pulled up. Though the effects of the development are localized, the natural character of the area is changed. The litter has attracted crows and gulls that wouldn't normally live up here, and they are an added problem for ground-nesting birds like ptarmigan.

The chairlift runs all year round, except in the roughest weather, and in summer takes up to 1000 people a day on to the now badly eroded summit of Cairngorm, and the great, wild plateau beyond. Although many are content to remain near the top, take pictures of one another and admire the view, this particular wilderness is now accessible to people who may not be used to mountain country and its dangers. The plateau can be savage enough during a summer storm, but in winter

The summit of Cairngorm, a popular destination for
wilderness-seekers in early summer.

there is a not infrequent condition known as white-out, which can be psychologically devastating as well as physically exhausting. In a white-out, there is no shadow, the horizon disappears and you can only see what is under your nose. Although in some ways white-outs are the opposite of darkness, in other ways they are very like it, and if you cannot navigate by compass you are lost. Syd Scroggie remembers how one particular light-hearted trip to the plateau on New Year's Day ended.

> We hadn't gone far when we realized we weren't going much further. It was wild white-out conditions, not falling snow but driven snow, whipped up by the gale. We made our way down by compass bearing to a little shelter where we put the tent up and decided we'd done enough for one day. The weather deteriorated further during the night, and next morning we realized we wouldn't be able to get down under our own steam, so we had to inch our way back to the chairlift through a Force 8 gale whitening everything out. You could only travel by compass, and even then only slowly and with great care, measuring our steps. We just managed to catch the last lift down before bad weather shut down the ski slopes.

A more insidious problem is posed by that icon of moor and glen, the red deer. There are few sights so stirring as a large herd of deer moving majestically across the bare hillside. There is the drama of the rut, the bull-roaring from the heather, and the clash of rival antlers. There is the deer's uncanny ability to forecast the weather, moving downhill in Indian file before the weather breaks, and passing back again before it improves. Duncan Matheson talks of how the great Gaelic poet, Duncan McIntyre, a humble stalker all his life, captures in simple words the grandeur of the 'branchy crested race', the steam of their breath on a frosty morning, their 'proud pace' 'brushing the dewy hay' in the morning. Only in Gaelic, the Highlander's native tongue, can he express fully his deep feelings about the land he loves and its finest wild beast.

How ironic that such an animal has become the central problem affecting wild Scotland today. Since the demise of the wolf, the red deer has had no natural predator; its numbers are controlled by shooting the surplus stock. But most Highland estates have become badly overstocked and, with deer nibbling every young tree in sight, the Highland woods are, quite literally, dying before our eyes. This is the quandary in which Dick Balharry finds himself as a conservationist.

We've only got two options: to reduce their numbers by shooting more of the hinds, or by putting up fences to keep them out of developing woodland. I prefer the former approach, because deer – red and roe – are an important part of the natural forest, so long as there is harmony between hungry mouths and the regenerating forest. At the moment, many Highland woods are full of old trees, and when they die the wood will disappear – like a city populated solely by ninety-year-olds. Some of the trees are dropping their last seed now, and it's vital that we do something to save these woods, so that we'll have something to show to our children, aye and their children too.

As Adam Watson adds, wryly: 'We're very fond of telling Brazilians how to look after their natural forest, and they're inclined to reply that you aren't making a very good job of looking after your own. I think it's time we made a better job of it.'

Wilderness changes you. When you meet people in remote places (whether you wish to see them or not) it seems natural to greet fellow spirits. Close companionships are forged from shared exertion and potential danger. At his adventure centre in Knoydart, Toby Robinson enjoys watching the gradual bonding between strangers. 'By the end of the week you've got a different person from the one that stepped off the boat from Mallaig. They've had an experience completely different from their normal life. They've had to live off their wits a bit, and live with the tides and the moods of the weather instead of fixed routines. When you see accountants and city people running down the hill all covered in mud and screaming with laughter, you feel a tremendous inner sense of satisfaction.'

Living in the wild changed Tom Rigg's relationship with the natural world.

I used to take part in the deer cull on the estate, and I never felt that went against nature, especially as, with modern rifles, the kill is usually quick and clean. But I don't shoot any more, and I've even given up fishing now because I can't stand the idea of hooks sticking in their throats. I don't want to hurt any animal now. I think those feelings come from living close to nature, all year round. When you wake up in the morning and see a fox outside your door, you do get a strong feeling of companionship with wildlife.

OVERLEAF The Cairngorm plateau in winter – one of the coldest and snowiest places south of the Arctic Circle and one of its few permanent inhabitants, a cock ptarmigan, the hardiest of all British birds.

Adam Watson believes that the growing sense that wilderness is not merely valuable but necessary lies at the root of contemporary attitudes towards conservation.

> Historically, we have been exploiters of wild areas, using them and changing them, but increasingly people have come to realize that it's important to have some wilderness left to remind us that man is part of the environment. We might need it for research, too, but the main need is more spiritual. There might even be a blood memory of our tribal ancestry involved, something in our genes. Primitive people often have intense religious feelings for the wild, the sense that they are part of it, that, for example, the Plains Indians in North America had. I think it's desirable to have areas where people feel in tune with nature and where, for once, they are not the most important part of the landscape. In that sense, wilderness means a lot to me. I have a deep respect for nature and the beauty of the natural world. As a scientist, I see that we are polluting or destroying a lot of the world, and I think man's desire to dominate the environment carries with it the seeds of his own destruction. So it's absolutely vital that we respect the shrinking amount of wild areas left and have a better regard to the other inhabitants that we share the world with.

In the end, we are back where we began, in the intensity of personal feeling of a man or woman alone among the hills. The search for wilderness is a quest for inner fulfilment, which people express in different ways.

> *I will attempt the cable track, old, stiff and retrograde,*
> *And get some pal to push me on, 'till resolution fade.*
> *For I must see black Meikle Pap against a starry sky,*
> *And watch the dawn from Lochnagar once more, before I die.*
> *The golden plover whistled there, before the Fall of Man,*
> *And you can hear the brittle croak of lonely ptarmigan.*
> *No heather there, but boulders bare, and quartz and granite-gripped,*
> *And ribs of snow, bleak cold and grey, as I remember it.*
> *And if I do not make the top, then sit me on a stone,*
> *Some lichened rock among the scree, and leave me there alone.*
> *Yes, leave me there alone to hear, where spout and buttress are,*
> *The breeze that stirs the little loch on silent Lochnagar.*

Anonymous poem found pinned to the door of a bothy in the Cairngorms.

INDEX

PICTURE CREDITS

BBC Books would like to thank the following for providing photographs and for permission to reproduce copyright material. While every effort has been made to trace and acknowledge all copyright holders, we would like to apologise should there have been any errors or omissions.

Anglia Press Agency 189; *Barnaby's Picture Library* 17, 36, 38, 47, 54; *Colin Baxter Photography Ltd* 94/95, 198; *The British Petroleum Company plc* 115; *R Clapperton* 157; *Bruce Coleman Ltd* 14/15, 138, 142 Hans Reinhard, 18 Felix Labhardt, 58(b), 74, 143 Dennis Green, 59, 79(l) Geoff Dore, 62 Eric Crichton, 79(r), 110, 190 Gunter Ziesler, 139, 207 Gordon Langsbury, 174 John Worrall, 195 Harald Lange; *Janette Eathorne* 42; *Phyllis Ellis* 194; *Marie Hartley* 135; *Hulton Deutsch* 20/21, 25, 30, 33, 41, 50, 67, 70/71, 86, 87; *Images Colour Library 90,* 118, 130/131; *Ian B Jones* 150/151; *Kent Messenger* 28/29; *Lewis Merthyr Band* 73; *Jim Meads* 182, 183; *Sir Anthony Milbank* 141; *Miss P R Miller* 177; *Mirror Syndication International* 10 Adam Woolfitt; *NHPA* 19 Alan Williams; *Nature Photographers Ltd* 106 Paul Sterry, 111 Hugh Miles, 211(b) Frank Blackburn; *OSF Ltd* 23, 102/103 Mark Hamblin, 163(b) Richard & Julia Kemp; *Penzance Library* 43, 46; *Joe Rock Photography* 167; *RSPB Photo Library* 58(t) M W Richards, 107, 179 C H Gomersall, 211(t) Richard Revels, 219(b) P J Newman; *Rural History Centre, University of Reading* 127, 129; *Scotland in Focus* 146 A G Johnston, 154 G Lockie, 159 Bob Lawson, 163(t) L Campbell, 170 J Forsyth, 202/203 J Weir, 215 B Chapple, 218/219 G Leaper; *Syd Scroggie* 200; *David Shale* 186, 187; *Shetland Museum* 101; *Edwin Smith* 112, 125; *Spectrum Colour Library* 78; *Topham Picture Point* 48, 97, 99, 120; *Bobby Tulloch* 105; *James T Walker* 164/165; *Adam Watson* 201; *Welsh Industrial & Maritime Museum* 64, 84.